D0045700

THE DEVIL'S
DOMINION

OTHER BOOKS BY THE SAME AUTHOR
Fiction
A Pocketful of Rye
The Seahorse
A Literary Lion
Conquering Heroes
The Syndicate

(As Richard Tate)
The Donor
The Dead Travel Fast
The Emperor on Ice
Birds of a Bloodied Feather

Nonfiction
The Natural History of the Vampire
The Summer That Bled: The Biography of Hannah Senesh
Bakunin: Father of Anarchism
Bedlam
Mind Map: An Investigation into Scientific Hand Analysis
Rosa Lewis: An Exceptional Edwardian
Marble Halls: The Biography of Mary Shiffer

Children's Books
The Jesus File
The Wind on the Heath
Voyage to Pluto

THE DEVIL'S DOMINION

By
Anthony Masters

The Complete Story of Hell and
Satanism in the Modern World

CASTLE BOOKS

This edition published in 2006 by
Castle Books ®
A division of Book Sales, Inc.
114 Northfield Avenue
Edison, NJ 08837

This book is reprinted with permission of
Peters Fraser & Dunlop, London.

Second Impression
First American Edition 1978

Copyright © 1978 Anthony Masters

All rights reserved.

No part of this publication may be reproduced, stored in
a retrieval system, or transmitted, in any form or by
any means, electronic, mechanical, photocopying,
recording or otherwise without the permission of the publisher.

Library of Congress Cataloging in Publication Data

Masters, Anthony, 1940-
  The Devil's dominion.
  Bibliography
  Includes index.
  1.   Devil. 2. Satanism. 3. Hell. I. Title

BF1548.M39   1978   133.4'22   78-14863

ISBN-13: 978-0-7858-2111-3
ISBN-10: 0-7858-2111-2

Printed in the United States of America

Contents

The Devil . . . is the product of belief in a God who is entirely good. He has his roots in Jewish tradition and his flowering in Christianity.

Dictionary of Witchcraft and Demonology

I think if the Devil doesn't exist, but man has created him, he has created him in his own image and likeness.

Feodor Dostoyevsky

On a starred night Prince Lucifer uprose
Tired of his dark dominion swung the fiend.

George Meredith

AUTHOR'S NOTE

This book is designed to assess both the ritual, artifacts and incidence of the Devil's dominion as well as a selection of those who practice Satanism and those who try to combat it. With reference to the latter I have quite deliberately concentrated on the last two centuries. I have not attempted to write a work of demonic history, but an account of how strong the demand for faith is—and how an alarming proportion of this demand is involved with the occult. Sometimes the text is ironic, at other times factual and in some instances philosophical. At all times it strikes the warning note that the Devil's dominion is not at the bottom of some mythical or Christian pit—but is surrounding us, both here on earth and in our minds. Milton, in *Paradise Lost*, says:

The mind is its own place, and in itself can make
a Heaven of Hell, a Hell of Heaven.

ANTHONY MASTERS
Sussex, 1978

PART ONE

The Administration

The most horrendous image of hell is Jean Paul Sartre's *Huis Clos*—where the characters face each other and their pasts eternally. The continuous repetition and their continual closeness is the greatest torture that could possibly be inflicted on them. But this claustrophobic misery is not the traditional vision of hell at all.

Every day thousands of us tell each other to go to hell. But having thus condemned our fellow human beings to purgatory, little thought is given to the exact nature, environment and hierarchy to which we would wish them dispatched. In fact, traditional hell, particularly that of the Christian tradition on which I'm going to concentrate, is a very specific world. The nature of hell is one of extremes, mainly of intense heat or intense cold. The sinner usually suffers both in varying degrees, depending on the strength of his sins. Father Joseph Hontheim* wrote in *The Catholic Encyclopedia* that:

*Professor of Dogmatic Theology, St. Ignatius College, Valkenburg, Holland.

11

Hell is a state of the greatest and most complete misfortune. After the last judgement there will be an increase of torment because subsequent to that event the demons and devils will never again be allowed to wander beyond the confines of hell, and thus restricted, will have only the miserable souls of the damned to torture and torment throughout all eternity.

Hontheim also tried to explain about hellfire and its longevity:

. . . According to the greater number of theologians the term *fire* denotes a material fire, and so a real fire. . . . Scripture and tradition speak again and again of the fires of Hell, and there is no sufficient reason for taking the term as a mere metaphor. . . . It is quite superfluous to add that the nature of Hell-fire is different from that of our ordinary fire; for instance it continues to burn without the need of a continually renewed supply of fuel. How are we to form a conception of that fire in detail remains quite undetermined; we merely know that it is corporeal.

In Mark, Chapter Nine, Verses 47 and 48, Mark writes that Jesus said:

And if thine eye offend thee, pluck it out: it is better for thee to enter into the Kingdom of God with one eye, than having two eyes to be cast into hell fire: Where their worm dieth not, and the fire is not quenched.

So the reality of hellfire is one upheld strongly by the Christian religion and from the Catholic point of view, the *Catholic Encyclopedia* firmly states that:

12

. . . the Church expressly teaches the eternity of the pains of Hell as a truth of faith which no one can deny or call in question without manifest heresy.

The pain and the permanent loneliness of hell, coupled with the sinners' total abandonment, represents an agony that man is unable ever to imagine. The Revelations also effectively warn those who worship the Devil that they will eventually:

. . . drink the wine of God's wrath, poured unmixed into the cup of his anger, and he shall be tormented with fire and brimstone in the presence of the holy angels and in the presence of the Lamb. And the smoke of their torment goes up for ever and ever; and they have no rest day and night.

Writing in 1565, St. Teresa of Avila claimed that she had visited hell to atone for her sins:

I felt a fire inside my soul, the nature of which is beyond my powers of description, and my physical tortures were intolerable. . . . But even this was nothing to my agony of soul, an oppression, a suffocation, and an affliction so agonizing that no words I could find would adequately describe it. To say that it was as if my soul were being continuously torn from my body is nothing. . . . I could not see my torturer, but I seemed to feel myself being burnt and dismembered; and I repeat, that interior fire and despair were the very worst of all.

Ice is also a satanic torture and it is the other major extreme to which the sinner is subjected in the traditional hell, although there is little mention of it in the Christian hell. Perhaps the most dramatic and awesome description of the hell of extremes lies in Dante's *Inferno*. This has nine layers and the deeper the sinner goes, the worse his fate. Lust, gluttony, avarice and prodigal waste are briskly dealt with in the first four layers. In the fifth layer the situation becomes more abrasive as those committed for the sin of anger are forced to tear each other to pieces, covered as they are with mud from the Styx (the mythological river of the Greek and Roman underworld). On the sixth layer all heretics are roasted in ovenlike tombs. On the seventh and eighth levels the situation becomes even more extreme with an assorted throng of so-called sinners being subjected to eternal barbarism. The categories include suicide, homosexuality, violence, fraud, theft, blasphemy, witchcraft, sorcery and lying. The tortures include the flogging of pimps and false lovers by demons, the immersion in excrement of flatterers, and the boiling in oil of the violent. Perhaps one of the most original of the tortures perpetrated on the seventh and eighth levels is that inflicted on suicides. These unfortunate miscreants are turned into trees whose leaves are torn apart and eaten by harpies.

But the most abysmal layer of Dante's *Inferno* is the ninth level. Here all traitors are lowered into the frozen lake of Cocytus and forced to spend eternity encased up to their necks in ice. In the center of the lake, Lucifer sits with ice up to his chest. He sprouts six enormous bat wings and he has three faces. One is yellow-white, one black and one red. In the central mouth Lucifer gnaws at Judas Iscariot, while his other mouths masticate Brutus and Cassius.

So the nature of hell is one of desperate extreme where every known punishment is meted out. Snake venom, excrement, burning flames, hail, snow, ice, nails, spikes, pits, branding, oil, pitch, sulphur, monsters, brimstone, flogging, eating alive, grinding, constriction, disease and laceration are among the most long-standing treatments meted out to sinners. But now a clear idea has been gained of the abuse the prospective sinner's body is to suffer—what of the environment of that suffering?

The geography of hell is both wild and Gothic. Black pits, bleak mountains, jagged cliffs, gloomy fortresses, rivers of blood or fire (sometimes both), junglelike dead woodlands, barren valleys, still lakes of deadly cold water or ice, swamps full of slime, vast lonely plains, deep caverns, sulphurous skies and an overall and overpowering stench would feature heavily in any satanic guidebook. These cruel features, the exact opposite of the grassy hills and flower-strewn meadows of heaven, are certainly complementary to the strenuous activity eternally taken among them.

Unfortunately, however, the prospective sinner is only given the vaguest possible indication as to the exact location of hell. The Bible, in such books as Numbers, Ezekiel and Philippians, talks about the earth opening up to receive the damned and it clearly defines hell as being underground—an abyss into which the wicked would descend. The Church is as vague as the Bible on the location of the abyss, and St. Chrysostom censoriously pointed out that "We must not ask where Hell is, but how we are to escape it." So basically the only guideline is that hell is somewhere below us and that it is geographically forbidding. As Richard Cavendish says in his book *The Powers of Evil,*

Hell is the ultimate and unsurpassable depth, the place furthest removed from sun and air and all the gentle warmth and beauty of life. Because it is the ultimate depth, it can also be considered fundamental, basic, essential, the foundation of everything above it.

15

Unspecified in its location, hell burns, as the hellfire preachers of the nineteenth century would have us think, below us all. It is, after all, the most logical place with its underground rivers and lakes—and, of course, molten fire. As souls fly upward to the pastoral eternity of heaven, the damned are drawn into the charnel house below.

So far we have seen the nature of the punishment inflicted on those sinners and the type of grim environment in which they are carried out. Now it is the turn of the satanic administration itself to come under scrutiny. Basically, the pecking order of the social levels of hell is quite complex. Much of the original belief comes from the Testament of Solomon, which gives details of the hierarchy from the earliest times and was originally reputed to have been given to Solomon by the vampire-demon Ornias. The legend goes that Ornias sucked so much blood from one of Solomon's slaves that Solomon asked God to intervene. God sent the Angel Raphael to him. Raphael gave Solomon a ring, the powers of which were such that it could dominate the entire range of demonry. Through the ring Solomon was able to discipline the administration—and conveniently to compile an inventory of its members. But this inventory was subject to enormous change, although by the seventeenth century a greater consistency emerged. By this time the hierarchy was divided into three, with Beelzebub as Crown Prince of Hell and Satan, or Lucifer as he was sometimes known, as First Lord.

The first hierarchy was ruled by Beelzebub and consisted only of devils (fallen angels). It contained Seraphim, still in the form of Holy Angels with six wings, Cherubim, still with wings, Rubens-type bodies and children's faces, and Thrones, with similar angelic forms if not hearts. Balberith as Prince of Cherubim, for instance, sowed the seeds of murder in humans' minds while his minions worked enthusiastically toward argument and blasphemy. Astaroth, Prince of Thrones, was responsible for idleness, laziness and lassitude while his minions initiated antagonism. There were many other aristocrats and their attendant departments.

The second hierarchy, ruled by Carreau, known as The Prince of Powers, consisted of dominions, principalities and powers. Among other temptations, this hierarchy specialized in eroding compassion and feelings of mercy.

The third hierarchy was dominated by Belios, Prince of Virtues, and this department was interested in arrogance and the mocking of God and the established Churches. Each hierarchy was further subdivided into all kinds of divisions of evil—in which the ordinary devils could apply themselves to any form of subversion that attracted them. Common, or garden, devils (or demons) were so thick on the ground in hell that once they inhabited a human being it was very difficult for any exorcising priest to identify them without calling upon them to state their name, rank and hierarchy—with which they often used to oblige.

Christian theologians chose a devil to represent each of the seven deadly sins. Among them were Satan for Anger, Belphegor for Sloth, Asmodeus for Lechery, Lucifer for Pride and Mammon for Avarice. But, as can be seen, these are mere ciphers and ignore completely the traditional hierarchies and the fact that Satan and Lucifer are one and the same.

The Christian hell also took in many devils or demons of other religions such as Baal, Eshmun, Moloch, Dagon and Astoroth. There were many demons of the air, of the wind and of the water, and in fact so vast was the administration of hell that when God agreed to let St. Macarius of Alexandria see Satan's hosts he saw them "as numerous as bees."

17

Finally the head of the administration—Satan. In Christian terms, Satan was originally a part of the heavenly administration, commanded by God to tempt men and women. At this stage no pact or bribe could be made with them. He was open only to the qualities of goodness. In Hebrew, Satan means adversary, and Satan's eventual banishment from heaven was a result of his becoming God's rival or adversary. Theologically, Persian thought influenced the Apocrypha into stating this pattern of events, and the New Testament takes for granted that Satan is an angel cast out of heaven for misconduct. The dualism of the Christian faith finds it essential to have very positive forms of heaven and hell, and Satan is the obvious choice to reign over hell. Released now from tempting to test goodness, Satan as monarch of hell has a much wider field, and his sole objective is to tempt into hell. Perverting the minds of the human race is the main campaign run by Satan and his demons and he has a number of weapons at his command, all of which are discussed in more detail in various parts of this book. Basically, however, they are the Pact, psychic powers, possession, witchcraft and eventually satanism.

But what tempted Satan out of Heaven? Milton provides the answer in *Paradise Lost*. "Better to reign in Hell than serve in Heaven." Even if Satan is only accepted as a mythological figure, this kind of temptation is very real. He is "an amalgam of pagan myth and latter day concept"* and on this basis is a convenient figure for theologians, to the writers of the Old and New Testament, and from one extreme of the established Church to the other. Simplification is all: Sinners unable to resist Satan will be cast into the fiery (or icy) pit. Those able to resist will be trumpeted through the gates of heaven, living eternal-

---

The Hierarchy of Hell, by Lauran Paine.

ly at peace with themselves, as well as with their friends and enemies. There is, of course, the third region—the no-man's land between heaven and hell where restless spirits dwell, sometimes breaking (or being forced into) human consciousness, at all times waiting for the Great Divider to give thumbs up or down.

The most dramatic account of the ejection of Satan (as the dragon) being cast out of heaven occurs in Revelations, Chapter 12, Verses 3–12:

> And there appeared another wonder in heaven; and behold a great red dragon, having seven heads and ten horns, and seven crowns upon his heads.
>
> And his tail drew the third part of the stars of heaven, and did cast them to the earth: and the dragon stood before the woman which was ready to be delivered, for to devour her child as soon as it was born.
>
> And she brought forth a man child, who was to rule all nations with a rod of iron: and her child was caught up unto God, and to his throne.
>
> And the woman fled into the wilderness where she hath a place prepared of God, that they should feed her there a thousand two hundred and threescore days.
>
> And there was war in heaven: Michael and his angels fought against the dragon: and the dragon fought and his angels.
>
> And prevailed not; neither was their place found any more in heaven.
>
> And the great dragon was cast out, that old serpent, called the Devil, and Satan, which deceiveth the whole world: he was cast out into the earth, and his angels were cast out with him.
>
> And I heard a loud voice saying in heaven, Now is come salvation, and strength, and the kingdom of

our God, and the power of his Christ: for the accuser of our brethren is cast down, which accused them before our God day and night.

And they overcame him by the blood of the Lamb, and by the word of their testimony; and they loved not their lives unto the death.

Therefore rejoice, ye heavens, and ye that dwell in them.

Woe to the inhabiters of the earth and of the sea! for the devil is come down unto you, having great wrath, because he knoweth that he hath but a short time.

Short time or not, Satan has established himself and his hierarchy as a massive force, whose powers are recognized by the Christian Church and, in some cases, are even exorcised with the official seal of approval. As a result, no greater work of public relations could have been better undertaken for Satan than the work done by the Christian Churches. In every sense they created him, epitomizing him as a deadly force of evil. By doing this, rather like antidrug posters illustrating a junkies' hideaway, they have made Satan both seductive and alluring.

To illustrate further the dualism that has created Satan, the word Devil was originally derived from the Greek word *Diabalos*, which means accuser. Demons (*Daemon*) meant friendly guardian spirits in the original Greek, but the use of the word, starting with the Septuagint, came to apply to evil idols and through the Latin became a name for evil spirits. Mixed in with all this chaotic terminology were the old pagan Gods. Asmodeus, Beelzebub (originally the God Baal Zebub to the ancient Phoenicians), Dagon, Leviathan, Belial and Behemoth all became part of the company of hell.

So it is clear that the satanic administration is an ethnic mix of vastly complex proportions. Into the melting pot has gone superstition, pagan religion, Christian religion, legend and fantasy. Out of it has emerged a figure of truly terrible proportions—Satan in all his different forms. Sometimes he appears in animal forms, sometimes as a half-man half-goat, which is partly based on the classical god Pan and partly based on the satyrs who enjoyed the downfall of Dionysus. Satan also appears as a full goat, usually black with a tail, cloven hooves and a red beard. Other times he appears as he might in the minds of painters and poets—with the ears of an ass, the horns of an ox, a body littered with ugly, grinning faces, a tail ending in serpents' jaws, goats' legs, feet like vultures' talons, and a coiled, razor-sharp penis. Occasionally Satan would appear in a more cunning and less formidable shape, and this is particularly illustrated in the poem "Quadriregio" written by the fourteenth-century Bishop Federigo Frezzi:

> Stately he was, and fair, and so benign
> His aspect, and with majesty so filled
> That of all reverence he appeared most worthy.

He was less worthy, however, in the eyes of those early saints who claimed to have had personal encounters with Satan. St. Guthlac (English Teetotaler) stated firmly that fire had gushed from every orifice, St. Fursey (an Irish Saint who founded monasteries and fell into trances) was certain that Satan's head resembled a brazen caldron, while St. Brigitta was convinced that Satan had feet in the form of grappling irons. Presumably this made it easier to enter nighttime bedchambers. Other sightings might be listed as follows:

21

The Blessed Gherardesca of Pisa: Saw Satan disguised as her husband.

Mary de Maillé: Saw Satan disguised as a much-respected holy man.

Henry II of the Holy Roman Empire: Saw Satan as a well-endowed young man sneaking away from his wife's bedroom.

St. Giles (French hermit): Saw Satan as an outsize tortoise.

Pope Silvanus II: Saw Satan as a friendly dog.

Messrs. St. Patrick, St. Geoffrey, St. Bernard: Saw Satan as a fly, as a reptile and in a variety of different animal forms.

Satan's personality is distinctly astringent. Having failed to tempt Job in the Old Testament (while operating from heaven) and having failed to tempt Jesus (now operating from hell), Satan's temperament is one of a major depressive. As the *Encyclopedia Americana* states:

Lucifer saw the splendor of his own angelic nature, together with its supernatural gifts, and rightly prized it. However, he wished to be sufficient unto himself and refused to admit that he depended on God and could find happiness only in God. His sin of rebellious pride was an act of complete egoism and pure malice: he loved himself to the exclusion of all else and without the excuse of ignorance, error, passion or weakness of will. The sin of the other rebel angels was likewise one of pride in themselves and perhaps in their leader.

Because of the perfection of the angelic will, Satan's choice, once made, was irrevocable. His rejection of God was eternal as is his subsequent punishment. His essential and greatest torment is the pain of loss, namely the loss of God by whom and for whom he was created. He is in utter despair and is filled with hatred for God, the good angels, mankind and his fellow demons.

Nevertheless, despite his disastrous psychological state, Satan has tremendous motivation, well described in 1684 in Richard Bovet's *Pandaemonium*.

Since the defection of the Fallen Angels from the first rectitude, or state of sublime Happiness and Glory . . . the indefatigable Enemy of Souls hath been restless in his Attempts to advance his own Infernal Dominion, and for the withdrawing Human Souls from that glorious Felicity, from whence himself and his Confederate Angels are for ever excluded. And to carry on this Diabolical design, no Fraud nor Artifice hath been omitted, no Delusions nor Suggestions neglected, no Temptations nor Allurements spared, that might entrap and enslave the ever-existing souls of man . . . For though he changed the highest Heaven for the Lowest Hell, a Palace of Eternal Happiness for a Dungeon of Eternal Horror, yet he changed not his Dire and Diabolical Resolutions: but still fights against the Thunder of the Almighty, and though vanquished, still retains his Traitorous Principle and inclination to Rebel.

Using all his powers, Satan's main tactics are to try to buy human souls at a high price (particularly for the seller). A surprising number of popes have sold him their souls, as well as such notables as Sir Francis Drake, who sold his soul in exchange for the position of admiral. Monks and nuns also seemed to have become involved in the negotiations—as have a variety of poets. Temptation, with money or sex, creating pride, possession, the link with witchcraft and satanic worship are the other wide areas in which Satan is able to work successfully. Nor does Satan always have to initiate—he is often summoned up by desperate mortals who want at most a pact and at least some help for a number of different reasons. Naturally Satan is not always victorious and is often defeated (amid enormous publicity) by exorcism. Less conventional methods have been known to work, as in the case of St. Anthony, who spat in Satan's face and even more strangely, the Abbot of Cluny, who drove him by the sign of the cross to seek protection in a gentlemen's lavatory.

Satanic attacks have been standard practice throughout the centuries, although these take a variety of different forms. St. Teresa of Avila mentions in her dramatic autobiography that her prayers were continuously interrupted by the Devil and her serious thought was replaced by nonsense. She also endowed Satan with bad temper and false humility. At one point Satan visited her, and St. Teresa described him vividly:

> A great flame seemed to issue from his body, which was intensely bright and cast no shadow. He said to me in a dreadful voice that I had indeed escaped his clutches, but that he would capture me still.

Other appearances include a hideously deformed bird that flew into the room of Elizabeth Barton, the Holy Maid of Kent, in 1534, as a tree covered with hoarfrost

24

and reeking of corruption to a Cistercian lay brother in 1363 and as a spider to the German visionary Christina von Stommeln in the thirteenth century.

Apart from the ill-assorted hellish administration, Satan also has a private life—of legendary sorts. The ancient Jewish religion claimed that he had four wives, and eleventh-century Christian thought considered that Satan could procreate. St. Thomas Aquinas, however, as well as St. Bonaventura, insisted that he was sterile—and there was only one way that he was able to procreate. This was to disguise himself as a woman, have sexual intercourse with a man, receive his sperm, turn himself back into a man—and then have sexual intercourse with a woman. A highly complicated and exhausting process.

On a more vicarious level, Satan often turns himself into an incubus (an evil spirit that has sexual intercourse with sleeping women) or a succubus (an evil spirit assuming female shape to have sexual intercourse with a man). Not unnaturally Satan's sexual victims have either gone mad or died awesome, bloated deaths a few days after the sexual act. Satan is a much more profound lover with his more natural choice of lover—the witch. Although never known to have taken one of them on as a wife, he has as many casual relationships with them as possible.

Finally there is no question of Satan's reformation. Eternally damned, he has been surrounded by priests, monks, nuns and other venerable beings, all of whom have been anxious to save him—and to bring him to God again. All have singularly failed. St. Hypatius actually went so far as to ask Satan why he did not at least try for repentance—but was told that as far as Satan was concerned, he considered he had never sinned in the first place.

As Lucifer, in Byron's poem "Cain," Satan makes his position absolutely clear:

> Through all eternity
> And the unfathomable gulfs of Hades,
> And the interminable realms of space,
> And the infinity of endless ages,
> All, all, will I dispute! And world by world,
> And star by star, and universe by universe
> Shall tremble in the balance, till the great
> Conflict shall cease, if ever it shall cease,
> Which it ne'er shall, till He or I be quenched.

Satan's name in heaven had been Lucifer, which means light-bearer. On earth it was Satan. Ringing in his ears throughout his demonic rule must be the famous words from Isaiah, Chapter 14, which predicted the imminent doom of the King of Babylon, but which St. Augustine took as referring to the heavenly battle and Satan's exile on earth:

> How art thous fallen from heaven, O Lucifer, son of the morning! How art thous cut down to the ground, which didst weaken the nations!

Satan's power was at its peak in the Middle Ages. Since then it has languished. But the 1970s have seen a new strengthening—and this has largely come about with loss of belief. While the established Christian Church loses thousands of believers, thousands of small cults of every extreme of belief are springing up. Man needs to believe. It is an instinct. And this is why that final area of Satan's influence—satanism—is growing. Out of a hotchpotch of romantic, religious and legendary drivel, a truly evil, menacing and dangerous situation is arising.

Satanic worshipers do not regard the Devil as evil. They regard him as an enemy of Christianity—a good and benevolent God who can only bring bounty to his worshipers—and can certainly never harm them, providing they toe the line. However, when a satanist uses the word "good" he does not use it in the same sense as the Christian means it. Satanists believe that Christian "good" is evil and vice-versa. They renounce the words of God and Christ and take pleasure in disobeying every possible commandment and guideline. Total self-indulgence is the satanic rule and each satanist is obliged to do the very opposite of Christianity and lead as anti-Christian a life as possible.

Crowley, Manson and those practicing more organized forms of satanism, such as Anton Sandor La Vey, who began the Church of Satan in San Francisco, have led the revival. So too has the obsession with possession and exorcism—beliefs that have split the Christian Church and rendered it wholly indecisive. "Do unto others as they do unto you" is La Vey's philosophy, and indeed this would be heavily endorsed by Satan himself. In a material, permissive, overreactive age, with the institutionalised Church in a state of flux, the satanist policy of turning Christian morality upside down is a very easy goal to achieve.

Crowley was brought up against a background of Victorian religious ideals which he delighted in rejecting. Manson failed against a background of the American dream—which he also delighted in rejecting. Those who need to be possessed *will* be possessed—and many an empty life has become meaningful and important as a result. Yet even satanists have clung to ritual. Crowley and Manson were dominated by ritual—and ritual plays a vital part in exorcism. This ritual must be housed, and satanic temples have abounded through the centuries, ranging from the kitsch of Dashwood's Hell-Fire caves to the directly sinister, such as this extract from an Italian newspaper describing a satanic chapel discovered in the Pallazzo Borghese in 1895. It was translated by Montague Summers in his *History of Witchcraft and Demonology:*

> The walls were hung all round from ceiling to floor with heavy curtains of silk damask, scarlet and black, excluding the light: at the further end there stretched a large tapestry upon which was woven in more than life-size a figure of Lucifer, colossal, triumphant, dominating the whole. Exactly beneath an altar had been built, amply furnished for the liturgy of hell: candles, vessels, rituals, missal, nothing was lacking. Cushioned prie-dieus (kneeling desks) and luxurious chairs, crimson and gold, were set in order for the assistants; the chamber being lit by electricity . . . arranged so as to glare from an enormous eye.

But in all reality it is not the satanists themselves who are as dangerous as the faithless, materialistic minds of ordinary mankind. If Satan is to propagate his works fully it must be to the most receptive. And the most receptive are the empty, the purposeless and the vicarious. That accounts for many of us. One of Satan's goals is that we should destroy ourselves, and we are already well on the way to achieving that. But his main objective is to destroy God through mankind by perverting or destroying belief. Judging by the state of disarray within the administration of the Christian Church in the Western World, the redundant, empty buildings and the dwindling congregations, it would also seem that we are well on the way to achieving this too. Sooner than we think, Satan may fulfill his final, long-awaited ambition. He will rule.

PART TWO

Welcome to Hell

There are no clocks in Hell, but an Eternal ticking.

Bridaine

In many ways this chapter is a diversion—a guide-book to hell that further enlarges on the sights and entertainments provided. But it is also a compendium of the way the Church, literature and art have seen this region over the centuries.

IT'S HELL—AT THE CENTER OF THE EARTH

Welcome to Hell from the entertainments manager and commander in chief Put Satanachia.

I take the greatest pleasure in welcoming you to hell on behalf of our administrator and my many colleagues. Before I take you on a guided tour it may interest you to know that we have a population of countless millions, many of whom you will shortly see busy with their own damnation. We have full tourist facilities, a varied land-scape and some of the most striking scenery to be found anywhere on earth—and certainly nowhere in heaven. We would warn the visitor that it is not considered poli-tic to mention this latter environment, and indeed penal-ties must be extracted under hellish legislation for any verbal slip in this direction. May I also remind you our population is sensitive to outsiders and keen to be re-lieved of their various tasks and occupations. Needless to say interference of any kind with our resident population is also prosecutable under hellish law.

Now let our tour begin to the various levels and depths of our beautiful region. As most of it has been created from the minds of men, I'm sure you will value source reference along the way. Jerome said that hell was like a huge winepress and you can just make out the beginning of this over on the hills above the mist. In the forest we have Augustine's ferocious flesh-eating animals which continually tear human beings to pieces, and Adam Sco-tus's boiling molten gold are on the plains below where our inhabitants are also beaten with red-hot brazen ham-mers.

Now we're drifting through a particularly interesting area, situated just below the fire hills. Here you can see the damned of Rochard Rolle's Stimulus Conscientiae, who tear and eat their own flesh, drink the gall of dragons and the venom of asps and suck the heads of adders. And if you care to examine their bedding and clothing you will find it consists of "horrible venomous vermin." As you can probably see, their diet is of note, nourishment being green bread washed down with an eggcupful of stinking water.

As we climb towards the fire hills I would like to draw your attention to the German sector just below us on the left. The whole sector is only one square mile into which

30

we've managed to squeeze a hundred million damned souls, which I think is something of a record. Their energies are devoted to being like grapes in a press, bricks in a furnace, salt sediment in a barrel of pickled fish and sheep in a slaughterhouse. You can probably hear them now. Over to the right is the French sector, which is less spectacular and more psychological. If you listen carefully downwind of the slaughterhouse you can probably hear the ticking. This is clearly of great novelty value as we have no clocks installed. Just the ticking.

Visitors are, of course, impervious to the flames so you can cross the fire hills with impunity. Our own inhabitants naturally burn at all hours. As we come through the last of the smoke no doubt you can make out the lake of pitch and brimstone just on the horizon. But just below us is Liguori's hell from his book *The Eternal Truths*, published as I am sure you will remember in 1758. The poster on that limb stretcher over there gives us a vivid description of Liguori's purgatory. Please note the actions of this colony of our inhabitants as I read the text.

> . . . The unhappy wretch will be surrounded by fire like wood in a furnace. He will find an abyss of fire below, an abyss above, and an abyss on every side. If he touches, if he sees, if he breathes, he touches, sees, breathes only fire. He will be in fire like a fish in water. This fire will not only surround the damned, but it will enter into his bowels to torment him. His body will become all fire, so that the bowels within him will burn, his heart will burn in his bosom, his brains in his head, his blood in his veins, even the marrow in his bones: each reprobate will in himself become a furnace of fire.

I think you will agree this is one of our most memora-

31

ble sights, and I know his Satanic Majesty delights in casually dropping in to see this spectacular torment. Another sector he is particularly interested in is the children's hell, which is just at the top of the glacier over there. Please also note the interesting extremes of climate and geographic feature we have here.

The children's hell, as you can see through these binoculars, is a particularly imaginative feature. It is mainly based on the Reverend Joseph Furniss's Victorian children's books about hell, in particular the one entitled *The Sight of Hell*. As you can see, there are streams of burning pitch and sulphur, deluged with sparks and an overall fire. To our right we have tormented souls roaring like dragons, hissing like serpents, howling like dogs and wailing like dragons. In the background you can see Furniss's six dungeons, each of which contains a child and an appropriate torture. They contain from left to right a burning press, a deep pit, a red-hot floor, a boiling kettle, a red-hot oven and a red-hot coffin. Our brochure contains an extract from *The Sight of Hell*, which was included at the specific request of our grand duke and counselor of fallen angels, Astaroth. If you'll permit me, I'll read you a short section while you watch that group of under-twelves being consumed by fire.

The little child is in the red-hot oven. Hear how it screams to come out; see how it turns and twists itself about in the fire. It beats its head against the roof of the oven. It stamps its little feet on the floor.

In the next valley we find Dante's Inferno, which I know you are all familiar with. If we can just drift over this batch of tormented souls I can conclude my brief guided tour with an aerial view. If you can take a locust each and draw yourselves well up into the saddle, we'll see a much larger area of our ever-changing region laid out below. As you can see we're now flying over the Hills of Despair, after which you can see the vast plain that is gradually opening up before you. Here our master is particularly delighted with the imagination of men and women up and down the ages for providing him with so many original ideas. Cheek by jowl, you can now see a cluster of hells, nestling together in cozy proximity.

In the foreground, for instance, we have an early Christian hell—a very fine example. Note the blasphemers hanging over the pyre by their tongues, the beating and lacerating of deflowered girls, the perpetual testicle kicking of masturbators, the adulterous women hung by their hair above boiling and bubbling mud, the milk congealing from the breasts of mothers who have murdered their offspring, the wicked rich being rolled to and fro over sharp stones, and many more interesting sights. A little to the left we can now see the hell of extremes, and despite the mist you can probably make out the human souls there jumping from the torment of the heat on the ground into the agony of the ice in the lake and back again. Repeatedly.

In the swamps in the center of the plain you can see further torture, and you can see the River of Blood is literally crammed with bathers today. On the foothills you can see the infernal workshops of Hieronymus Bosch, and just above the grim towers and battlements of the castle we find John Custances's hell, where, and I quote

> the ego is . . . increasingly restricted, until it seems to become an almost infinitesimal point of abject misery, disgust, pain and fear. It is very noticeable that the repulsion is not only felt for the outside

33

world; it invades the personality in the form of intense disgust for oneself, horror of one's body, of seeing one's reflection in a mirror.

Higher up you have an excellent view of James Joyce's hell. You can see the high walls of his foul-smelling prison with its demon jailers, and you can probably see the smoke and flames belching out of the windows. Our schedule doesn't allow a visit to the interior, but I assure you it is another classic hell of its type. The damned are quite helpless in there, and indeed they haven't even the strength to remove from their eyes worms that regularly gnaw at the pupils. They lie in the filth of all the world, and their own bodies are so contaminated with pestilence that if we allowed any individual out they would infect the whole world. They are, of course, trapped by fire of considerable intensity as well as by the presence of the demons and their hatred of each other.

On our right there is another children's hell, once again beautifully conceived by Mrs. Sherwood, who wrote *The History of Susan Gray*—a children's novel which held up our own beloved region as a deterrent to working-class attitudes and general misbehavior. As we fly over you can see exactly what Mrs. Sherwood meant when she wrote:

> Children who play in the streets with others learn to lie and to swear, and perhaps to steal. They grow up to be idle, bold, bad men and women; and when they die, they go to a place where they live with devils in fire and brimstone, and chains and darkness.

Now we are coming toward the end of our tour. Far up on the top of the Mountains of Purgatory you can see

John Bromyard's Dominican hell—a marvelous antiquity from the fourteenth century and known to be a collectors' item. Those entering Bromyard's hell were kings, lords, judges, lawyers, usurers, evil churchmen, the rich, powerful and sinful, the haughty, the lustful, the gluttonous and the envious. On the mountaintop you can now see the deep lake which is Bromyard's hell. At the bottom of the lake there is a narrow pit for each body, and in each pit a bath of pitch and sulphur. Their beds are made of nails and spikes, and each time they embrace each other (which they are regularly forced to do) they burn. No wives are allowed, but marriage is arranged with toads. Neither are acolytes or servants allowed, and these are replaced by a great crowd of worms.

A glorious point at which to end our brief guide to the hellish regions. Of course you have seen but a fraction of the deadly torment we offer. We must, of course, express our deep gratitude to those human beings who have invented such delightful purgatories for us, and we hope we have done them justice by displaying so lavishly here in hell. May I leave you with two visions. One from Dante's Inferno at the ninth level.

> Even a cask, through loss of middle-piece or cant, yawns not so wide as one I saw, ripped from the chin down to the part that utters vilest sound; between his legs the entrails hung; the pluck appeared, and the wretched sack that makes excrement of what it swallowed.
>
> Whilst I stood all occupied in seeing him, he looked at me, and with his hands opened his breast saying "Now see how I dilacerate myself, see how Mahomet is mangled! Before me Ali weeping goes, cleft in the face from chin to forlock;

"And all the others, whom thou seest here, were in their lifetime sowers of scandal and of schism; and therefore are they thus cleft.

"A devil is here behind, who splits us thus cruelly, reapplying each of this class to his sword's edge, when we have wandered round the doleful road; for the wounds heal up ere any goes again before him."

A good example of our versatility. As you will have seen the damned in this case were being split down the middle for dividing Christianity.

Our second vision is a profane one—a vision that you are much privileged to see on your short visit to hell. It is a vision of Satan himself, created by John Milton in *Paradise Lost*:

> The other shape,
> If shape it might be call'd that shape had none
> Distinguishable in member, joint or limb,
> Or substance might be call'd that shadow seem'd,
> Fierce as the Furies, terrible as Hell.

So even our master is grateful to those who imagined his form so dramatically. The tour is now over, pacts can be made on your way out if so desired, and please remember you are welcome to hell. Anytime.

PART THREE

Hell On Earth

You have the Devil underrated
I cannot yet persuaded be,
A fellow who is all behated
Must something be!

Goethe

On a more serious level, hell has been made manifest on earth many times. This was convenient to the Church, largely because an apparent sighting gave further credibility to the existence of hell itself. It was all very well to preach hellfire from the pulpit, but the sinful would be far more prone to repentance and obedience if Satan or any of his hierarchy appeared on earth. Of course the most powerful appearances were through possession or witchcraft which are dealt with later. This part of the book is particularly concerned with hell itself and the satanic hosts visiting earth—through the all-too-welcoming minds of mankind. These minds had been indoc-

37

trinated with the idea that hell was exactly as we have just seen it.

As the Christian Church grew in the Western World and became more powerful, so did Satan as the major adversary to God. It was the policy of heaven that Satan should work evil, and his claims on lost souls were a vital deterrent to sinners. The kingdom of hell was a far more easily recognizable place than the kingdom of heaven, which most people found very hard to imagine indeed. The priests gave only the barest indications as to its pleasantries and quite often made it sound an eternity of boredom. Heavenly gates, St. Peter, the angels, harps, clouds and eternal love and peace were the principal features, but there were few other identifying factors. Certainly it would be quite impossible to compile the same kind of detailed guide as I have just done for hell, which has so many identifiable and diverse features.

Hell on earth principally involves various forms of temptation. These are either seen as visions or actually interpreted by practicing satanists. I'll take the visions first. Like gossip or anecdote, these started from one source and having passed through thousands of other sources and also through some hundreds of years, they have become both magnified and distorted. The most famous temptation, and certainly one of the most grueling, was the temptation of St. Anthony. It is also the classic case-history from which so much inspiration arose for both vision and legend.

St. Anthony was born in Egypt around 250 A.D. His biographer, St. Athanasius, writing in the following century, said that he was brought up in the Christian faith by wealthy parents. Considered to be too devout and too sensitive to join the hurly-burly of school life, he remained illiterate. At twenty, his parents died and St. Anthony lived entirely alone. As his biographer puts it:

He took no care for anything whatsoever except his soul, and he began to train himself in the habits of the strictest abstinence and self-denial.

Satan took St. Anthony on as his biggest early challenge, trying to break the abrasive routines that the future saint was carrying out. At first some by now very familiar tactics were tried. "Filthy and maddening" thoughts entered St. Anthony's mind, and he was continuously pestered with material and worldly worries. But this failed to interfere with his diet of bread, salt and water, his continuous fasting and deliberate sleeplessness. Satan then appeared to St. Anthony as a woman, but the seduction was doomed to failure from the start.

Stepping up his own counterattack, St. Anthony moved into a tomb, but was there attacked by a diverse number of demons. St. Athanasius writes:

One had the form of a lion and another had the appearance of a wolf and another was like unto a panther and all of the others were in the forms and similitudes of serpents and vipers and scorpions. The lion was roaring as a lion roars when he is about slay; the bull was ready to gore with his horns; the panther was prepared to spring; and the snakes and the vipers were hissing, and they appeared to be in the act of hurling themselves upon him; the sounds which they made and the forms in which they showed themselves were terrible.

St. Athanasius goes on to point out that St. Anthony was relatively undisturbed by Satan's onslaught—"his mind remained wholly undisturbed. And as he was lying down he laughed at these phantoms." Recently, however, the grim voice of reality has been suggesting that the saint may well have been eating bread infected by a fungus called *Claviceps purpurea*, which contains lysergic acid on which LSD is based. But whether the visions were seen in a normal mind or a chemicalized mind seems of little importance. St. Anthony had built his life around resistance to Satan—and he was determined that a battle royal should take place to justify his physical privations. A few years later St. Anthony became a hermit, shutting himself away in an old fort where he continued his self-denial up until his death. He was surrounded (outside the fort) by a large number of disciples who continuously begged St. Anthony to teach them. Eventually he broke his hermitage and did as requested. But his self-denial and therefore his defense against Satan continued as extremely as before as the ever-detailed St. Athanasius points out: "He never touched his body with water . . . and he never dipped his feet in water without the sternest necessity."

Apart from activating the imaginations of thousands who also subconsciously sought the visions of hell, St. Anthony also stimulated the imaginations of many painters including, of course, the ferocious inventiveness of Hieronymous Bosch.

From the time of St. Anthony to the present day, hell has appeared in the minds of mankind countless millions of times. The sightings, however, have largely been made at night. The witch-hunt is one of the most common European visions of hell, although its real origins lie with either the German god Woden or the Scandinavian equivalent Odin—god of the dead and war who had a link with the Valkyries. The hunt rages across both earth and sky, a dramatic and demonic spectacle including a large pack of baying hounds, a shrieking huntsman and the cacophony of many horns. The riders could either be dead souls or demons, but either way a sighting of the hunt was an omen of death, disaster, war or some frightful catastrophe. On no account should the hunt ever be seen, and those who have heard it coming have inevitably thrown themselves on the ground and covered their eyes. The most foolhardy possible course of action was to speak to the hunt's leader. The conversation would be a short one—as instant death would result.

The Bible conveniently supports the notion that hell is abroad at night, and Psalm 91 says: "Thou shalt not be afraid for the terror by night nor for the pestilence that walketh in darkness." The pestilence includes owls, nightjars and bats—all of which are considered to be Satan in varying moods of surveillance or alternatively providing a premonition of impending evil. Curlews and geese are sometimes known as the Gabriel Hounds and Death Hounds, and are greatly feared in Northern Europe. But perhaps the most sinister (and the most prolific) sightings of hell on earth are the Seven Whistlers. These unidentifiable birds course the night sky, emitting an unearthly cry, and are said to be either the Jews, unable to be at peace after the crucifixion of Christ, unbaptized babies or the damned. If the birds are sea birds they are then considered to be the bodies of dead sailors. In all cases the chilling sound of the Seven Whistlers precedes death.

The toad is a more substantial expatriate from hell, that now resides here and is part of a permanent hellish settlement which includes wolves, goats, pigs, cats and ravens. (These are almost always the familiars of witches and as a result their demonology is described in a later chapter.) Milton, in *Paradise Lost*, tells how Satan turned himself into a toad in the Garden of Eden so that he could more conveniently sit by Eve's ear and slip into it poison to pollute her bloodstream. Legends abound concerning

41

the toad's link with witches, and, more widely, its link with Satan. In Devonshire, toads were burned because they were believed to be in league with him, while in Cambridgeshire toads were said to be able to predict storms. In the same county there were "toadmen" who had devilish power over horses and were able to make them either controllable or uncontrollable at whim. The last known record of the practice was as recent as 1938. To become a toadman it was necessary to skin a toad or alternatively to pin it to an anthill until its bones were picked clean. The aspiring toadman would carry the bones in his pocket until they were completely dry. Then, waiting for the full moon, he would plunge the bones into a stream at midnight. Directly they were immersed, the bones would scream aloud and one would drift off on its own. Providing he was able to rescue this bone, then the demonic league would be made and a fully fledged toadman would emerge.

Another satanic resident here on earth is the pig, largely as a result of the Christian religion. The New Testament recounts how demons, exorcised by Christ, entered the bodies of the Gadarene Swine. However, to illustrate once again the duality of the religion, there is a patron saint of swineherds who was named St. Anthony. In the North of England (Winwick and Burnley in Lancashire) there are two effigies of pigs carved on the two parish churches. The pig was considered to be particularly vulnerable to the evil eye in this area. Elsewhere, in both New England and Ireland, there was a strong legend concerning one of the more obscure of Satan's guises—the Black Boar.

The satanic menagerie was further swelled by the goat—always a sinister presence, and one of Satan's most familiar guises. Sexuality has always been the keynote of the goat. Lechery, stench and capriciousness are the three main associations with the animal, and all of these have been in turn associated with Satan. As pictured, Satan as a goat has great similarity to the amorous Greek god Pan, who had a human body with the ears, loins, legs and hooves of a goat. Much of the legend is concerned with the copulation between humans (usually witches) and the Devil. In Jewish folklore the Watchers (the fallen angels who sinned because of their sexual need for the daughters of humans) are another clue. Azazel, the leader of the Watchers, taught mankind to make weapons of war when he was exiled from heaven, relying on his link with Mars, the planet of war, for expertise. Azazel was also associated with the ritual of the Jewish scapegoat in which a goat was selected each year to represent the fallen angel himself. Heaped with the sins of the Jewish people, it was sent out into the wilderness to seek out its black master—Azazel. This probably influenced the medieval belief that witches enjoyed copulating with the Devil in goat-form, and Exodus 22 backs this up, at the same time giving credibility and justification to the witch-hunters.

Thou shalt not suffer a witch to live. Whosoever lieth with a beast shall surely be put to death. He that sacrificeth unto any god save the Lord only, he shall be utterly destroyed.

Because of this there were a large number of successful medieval prosecutions concerning "witches" having sexual intercourse with the Devil. The witches of Arras in 1460, for instance, claimed to have worshiped Satan in the form of a goat, "Then with candles in their hands they kiss the hind parts of the goat that is the Devil."

The wolf is also well known as a satanic figure, but is more of a familiar than a shape-changer. The animal is

43

also a means of transport for the Black Master to roam the earth, and German legend has it that the Devil sits between the eyes of the wolf. Another legend claims that the wolf was created by Satan, his heart from stone, his head from a stump of wood and his breast from the roots of a tree.

Mythological beasts also feature in the satanic presence on earth. These include the vampire, the dragon, horned demons and the great beast of the Antichrist. The vampire, his image blunted by too many twentieth-century film treatments, is an animated corpse. This hireling of Satan has a number of functions, the chief of which is to satisfy his own appetite for blood by gorging at the throats of the living. A shape-changer, the vampire can also change himself into a variety of nocturnal animals, the favorite of which is the wolf. He can also command a pack of wolves to do his bidding and is able to hypnotize his victims sufficiently so that they are powerless during his gory feast.

The dragon, in both the Old Testament and in the Jewish writings of the first century A.D., represents both desolation and mourning. In early Christian writings it represents either Satan himself or Satan's servant. As we have already seen, in the Book of Revelations the dragon is described as being large, red and with seven heads and ten horns. There then follows the battle between St. Michael and his angels—and the dragon, representing Satan, and his angels:

> And the great dragon was thrown down, that ancient serpent who is called the Devil and Satan, the deceiver of the whole world; he was thrown down to the earth, and his angels were thrown down with him.

There is another reference to the dragon in Isaiah:

> In that day the Lord with his hand and great and
> strong sword will punish Leviathan the fleeing ser-
> pent, Leviathan the twisting serpent, and he will slay
> the dragon that is in the sea.

Leviathan, or the dragon, is seen as God's earthly com-
batant—and it symbolizes Satan's presence on earth. In
fact, the whole visual concept of hell was probably inspired by God describing Leviathan to Job. Leviathan appeared to be an enormous supernatural crocodile with
certain whalelike characteristics. Flames leaped from its
jaws and smoke from its nostrils. This extraordinary apparition definitely influenced the medieval pictures
representing the mouth of hell—which was often depicted as the gaping and fiery mouth of Leviathan. Some art-
ists went further—and via Leviathan represented hell as a
boiling caldron in which sinners burn.

The horned Christian demon probably derived from
either the goat or from the bull-god of Mithraism. In the
seventeenth century a large number of so-called witches
in England claimed that Satan had appeared to them disguised as a bull. But it was as early as 447 A.D. when the
Theological Council of Toledo established the first definition of the Devil. They saw him as "a large black monstrous apparition with horns on his head, cloven
hooves . . . an immense phallus and a sulphurous
smell."

The final mythological beast of importance is the great
beast. Inextricably linked with the dragon and the Antichrist, the great beast represents the greatest concentra-
tion of hell on earth. It signifies the coming of the Apocalypse—just as the Antichrist signifies the coming of a
man, sometimes thought of as the Devil's son, who is the

evil opposite of Jesus Christ. Revelations, Chapter 13, describes the emergence of the great beast from the sea:

> And I stood upon the sand of the sea, and saw a beast rise up out of the sea having seven heads and ten horns, and upon his horns ten crowns, and upon his heads the name of blasphemy.
>
> And the beast which I saw was like unto a leopard, and his feet were as *the feet* of a bear and his mouth as the mouth of a lion: and the dragon gave him his power, and his seat, and great authority.
>
> And I saw one of his heads as it were wounded to death; and his deadly wound was healed: and all the world wondered after the beast.

The great beast dominated the earth for three and a half years and was worshiped. It was also joined by a second, subordinate beast whose arrival on earth was almost as striking as its master.

> And I beheld another beast coming up out of the earth; and he had two horns like a lamb, and he spake as a dragon.
>
> And he exerciseth all the power of the first beast before him, and causeth the earth and them which dwell therein to worship the first beast, whose deadly wound was healed.

This second beast also insisted that all worshipers of the great beast should be marked on the right hand or on their forehead

> And that no man may buy or sell, save he that had the mark, or the name of the beast or the number of his name.

Here is wisdom. Let him take that hath understanding count the number of the beast; for it is the
number of a man; and his number is six hundred
three score *and* six.

The number 666—the most enigmatic and sinister one
in the Bible. But in fact its real meaning, if the letters are
turned into numbers, could well be Nero. If his Greek title Neron Kaisar is translated into Hebrew, then the letters add up to 666. So the great beast, in the Revelations
at least, is Nero. Also, it is clear from the Revelations
that its author, St. John the Divine, regarded the great
beast as the Antichrist although he never used the actual
term. St. John calls the second beast the false prophet,
which is a reference to the false Christs and false prophets that Jesus spoke of who will show signs and wonders to lead the faithful astray.

In Chapter 7 of Daniel, the four Jew-oppressing em-
pires of Babylon, Media, Persia and Alexander the Great's
Greece are seen as four beasts in a vision.

Daniel spake and said, I saw in my vision by night,
and, behold the four winds of heaven strove upon the
great sea.

And four great beasts came up from the sea, diverse one from another.

The first was like a lion, and had eagle's wings: I
beheld till the wings thereof were plucked, and it
was lifted up from the earth, and made stand upon
the feet as a man, and a man's heart was given to it.

And behold another beast, a second, like to a bear,
and it raised up itself on one side, and it had three
ribs in the mouth of it between the teeth of it: and
they said thus unto it, Arise, devour much flesh.

After this I beheld, and lo another, like a leopard,

which had upon the back of it four wings of a fowl; the beast had also four heads; and dominion was given to it.

After this I saw in the night visions, and behold a fourth beast, dreadful and terrible, and strong exceedingly; and it had great iron teeth: it devoured and brake in pieces, and stamped the residue with the feet of it: and it was diverse from all the beasts that were before it; and it had ten horns.

I considered the horns, and, behold, there came up among them another little horn, before whom there were three of the first horns plucked up by the roots: and, behold in this horn were eyes like the eyes of man, and a mouth speaking great things.

In Chapter 12, Daniel states that the beasts' rule would last for "a time, times and a half," i.e., three and a half years. Then the power of the persecutor (Antiochus Epiphanes—the first human prototype for the Antichrist) would end.

Theologians accept that the great beast represents Rome, the oppressor of both the Christians and the Jews. The kind of worship required by it was that of the emperors, and the false prophets are the authorities responsible for furthering the totalitarianism of the emperors. There is other supportive evidence for this too, in that the great beast comes from the sea (meaning abroad as in the case of the emperors) and the false prophet, or subsidiary beast, from the earth (meaning from at home as in the case of the local authorities). Also, the seven heads of the great beast must represent both the seven Roman emperors and the seven hills of Rome. The graven images that the beast demanded to be erected probably refer to Caligula's demands in 30 A.D. that his statue be erected in the

Holy of Holies in Jerusalem—a sacrilege deliberately aimed at grossly offending the Jews. Finally, the mortal wound in one of the great beast's heads would appear to be a reference to the rumors that Nero, the great Christian persecutor who committed suicide in 68 A.D., was still alive and would return with an army eventually to conquer Rome.

During the course of Revelations, Chapters 19 and 20, a battle takes place between the great beast, the kings of the earth and their armies, and God's forces, the latter being led by The Word of God, a rider on a white horse.

> His eyes *were* as a flame of fire and on his head *were* many crowns: and he had a name written, that no man knew, but he himself.
>
> And he *was* clothed with a vesture dipped in blood: and his name is called The Word of God.

The great beast and his armies were heavily defeated and killed. The beast and the false prophet are then despatched to their last resting place.

> And the beast was taken, and with him the false prophet that wrought miracles before him, with which he deceived them that had received the mark of the beast, and them that worshipped his image. These both were cast alive into a lake of fire burning with brimstone.

Such was the fate of the great beast and his second-in-command, who is also said to be the Antichrist because of his being a false prophet and being able to display the "wonders" that led millions onto the satanic path. But despite the confusion over the identity of the Antichrist, it is important to realise that Mark tries to clarify the point by saying that the first beast was the false Christ—and the second the false prophet.

Ominously, Chapter 20 of Revelations prophesies the emergence of Satan from the pit into which the serpent, i.e., Satan himself, had been cast.

And when the thousand years are expired, Satan shall be loosed out of his prison.

So Satan has been among us for centuries. Only the final apocalypse could reincarnate his bestial allies. But their satanic presence lives on.

The Devil's greatest spiritual forces on earth are the incubus and the succubus. Both rely entirely on sexual guilt and are as easily introduced as desire. In fact they *are* desire and are only seen as devilish because of guilt. In fact it is the erosion of guilt that is satanic—not the sexual fantasies blamed on the highly convenient incubus and succubus. Erotic dreams and orgasm through masturbation have been blamed on these mythical forces throughout the centuries—as has the more indictable offense of vicarious, casual infidelity. Here the guilt is at least the weapon of punishment—which theologically takes the power from the hands of Satan—to the hands of God.

In satanics, an incubus was a demon that had sexual intercourse with women, while a succubus had sexual intercourse with men. The former were particularly active in nunneries, while in monasteries succubi proliferated. Albert Magnus pointed out that "there were places in which a man can scarcely sleep at night without a succubus accosting him." However, the Christian faith believed that there was no way a demon could create life.

50

They could, on the other hand, activate corpses, possess others or create a temporary materialization.

Both succubus and incubus are based on a number of legends, all of which are themselves based on the sexual desire and resultant guilt mentioned above. The medieval Jewish demoness Lilith, for instance, was one such predecessor. With a basically winged human form, she flew wailing through the night. She and her offspring not only seduced men while they slept, but also were vampiristic and sucked their blood. They also attacked newly born children and their mothers. Various precautions had to be taken against them, including protective circles and never leaving the objects of attack or seduction alone in the house. Jewish legend claimed that Lilith was Adam's first wife who left him before the more suppliant Eve was created. Her reasons for leaving him were those of emancipation—she refused to lie beneath him as instructed. She also considered herself his equal. God then apparently sent three angels to remonstrate with her but Lilith sourly refused to cooperate, pointing out that she considered her vocation in life was now to attack children. To show further rebellion she consistently had sexual intercourse with such a rich variety of demons that her own demon offspring were beginning to number thousands. As a result God ordered that at least a hundred of her children should be exterminated each day. A standard precaution to keep the ever marauding Lilith away from babies was to draw a magic circle around the child and to inscribe in charcoal "Adam and Eve barring Lilith." Also, the words "Sanvi, Sansanvi, Semangelaf" had to be written on the door—these being the names of the three angels God sent to appeal to Lilith. Unfortunately they had not been successful.

One interesting, and certainly alarming, reference in

51

Genesis, Chapter 5, Verse 3, states that Adam fathered, with Eve, a son "in his own likeness." There is a sinister implication here that in the past he had fathered children very far from his own likeness.

The Lamia, of Greek and Roman folklore, were also predecessors of the incubus and succubus. Like the Lilith, the Lamia attacked children and seduced sleeping men—and in these days of promiscuity and child-beating it would seem that the Lilith and the Lamia were inventions of man's own eternal sexual dilemma—and eternal chauvinism. The Lamia wished to absorb their victims' life-energy. Both the Lamia and the Lilith were identified when the Old Testament was translated into Latin. In Isaiah the original verse referred to Lilith and was translated *Ibt cubavit lamia et invenit sibt requiem.* In the Authorised Version the phrase becomes: "The screech-owl also shall rest there, and find for herself a place of rest."

But the legends had their place in reality, for many of them were based on the frustration of women unable to have children—or those who had had them taken away. Therefore, the cannibalistic "appetite" of the Lilith and Lamia for the flesh of young children was largely a symbol of this frustration. The legends tended to be at their most prolific in times of high child-mortality rates.

Promiscuity also made the Lilith, the Lamia and their demonic followers—the incubus and the succubus—more than acceptable. Genuine lovers were often passed off as incubi or succubi, and one medieval nun claimed that she had been sexually assaulted by no less a devout than the Bishop Silvanus. The bishop, however, hastily claimed that the attack was nothing whatsoever to do with him but was an incubus who had appeared in his form. It was obviously difficult to refute this alarming statement.

52

Uncontrolled sexuality was one of the most immediate means of being consumed in hellfire, and so little wonder that Satan's most positive earth forces were the demon lovers. As can be seen later in this chapter, belief in the incubus and succubus was maintained well into the twentieth century. Aleister Crowley, for instance, wrote that seed spilled in masturbation, nocturnal emission or coitus interruptus did not go to waste. The energy was used by incubi and succubi.

> The ancient Jewish Rabbins knew this and taught that before Eve was given to Adam the demon Lilith was conceived by the spilth of his dreams, so that the hybrid races of satyrs, elves and the like began to populate those secret places of the earth which are not sensible by the organs of the normal man.

There are various satanic supports given to his spawn on earth. These include curses, poisonous plants, and such artifacts as the "hand of glory."

Once you believe you are going to die, you probably will. Man's willpower has often been proven to be stronger than his body. Conversely, many have recovered from serious illness by sheer willpower. God can curse as much as the Devil can. Adam and Eve were cursed when they were expelled from the Garden of Eden. Excommunication is known as cursing by bell, book and candle; the bell was tolled as if the excommunicant were dead, the curse was read from the closed book, and candles were snuffed out. This symbolized the removal of the offender's soul from the sight of God. Anti-grave robbing measures were also taken on a Christian basis, and Shakespeare's epitaph on his Stratford tomb reads:

Good friend, for Jesus' sake forbear
To dig the dust enclosed here.
Blest be the man that spares these stones
And curst be he that moves my bones.

But outside Christianity, Satan has a battery of curses lined up for various different earthly situations. A selective choice is as follows:

(a) Taking the Lord's name in vain at all possible times.
(b) Using the words "hell" and "damnation" as much as possible.
(c) Casting death spells from sorcerers and witch doctors to primitive victims and relying on the psychology of the situation to damn the victim.
(d) Creating a malevolent wish in the mind against a potential victim (the "ill-wishing" of witchcraft fame).
(e) Publicly cursing livestock.
(f) Casting the evil eye.
(g) Making a doll in the image of the victim and piercing it with sharp objects, hoping to cause the subject acute pain.
(h) Invoking the ghosts of one's ancestors to bring sickness on an erring relative.
(i) Hereditary curses to which generations of a family may succumb.

Satanically, cursing is a double weapon. Not only is it highly effective to the curser and the cursed—but other demonic use can be made of it. A lighthearted example of this is the cursing well of St. Elian at Llanelian-yn-Rhos, near Colwyn Bay in Wales. This was a great commercial success on two levels. The curser would write the name of an enemy on a piece of paper, place it in a lead box and fasten it to a slate on which the curser's initials were written. The contraption was then given to the wellkeeper and a fee was also given to him. This custodian then recited the curse—and the lead box was thrown into the depths of the well.

The victims, however, were also in a position to alleviate themselves of the curse and, providing they knew it was in the notorious well, they would hurry to it. Having paid the keeper the appropriate fee, the following ceremony would then be performed. The keeper would read aloud two psalms to the intended victim—and would then ask him to walk around the well three times. The curse would then be drawn up from the well, the lead box opened—and the written curse handed over. The curser was, of course, at liberty to return and put the curse down the well again—and the victim could then once again extract it. The two contrasting ceremonies could be repeated endlessly and the keeper was more than amicable to the process. Business was reported to be continuously brisk.

Tribal cursing still continues today, but it is not unknown in more civilized areas. In 1953 an Arizona rancher shot and killed a woman who everyone thought had put a curse on his wife. In 1964 a German farmer, seeing his livestock dying around him, accused his wife of putting a curse on them. It must be noted that in the majority of curse situations, it is either the nearest and dearest who is being cursed, or the nearest and dearest who is doing the cursing.

Poisonous plants have always been considered to be another part of Satan's dominion on earth. With bright, seductive colors or berries, they would lure the naive towards them—and still do. Here is a checklist of the more noxious:

(a) Herb Paris (*Paris Quadrifolio*). Poisonous. Tastes bitter. Causes diarrhea. Unusual regular cross-pattern with four leaves, a flower of four inner and four outer divisions, and eventually a shiny black berry at its center.

(b) Nightshade (*Solenum Dulcamara*). Slightly poisonous. Tastes bittersweet. Used as a protection against the evil eye.

(c) Blackthorn and hawthorn. Bad luck in the house. Also used as protective device.

(d) Yarrow. Plant dedicated to the Devil.

(e) Deadly nightshade (*Atropa Belladonna*). Very poisonous indeed. To be taken by potential visionaries or fortune tellers—providing they survived to use the magic, which is unlikely. Also made into potions to drive victims mad or to kill them.

(f) Henbane (*Hyoscyamus niger*). A close relative of the deadly nightshade. Equally poisonous but lacks the luscious-looking berries. Has a nauseating smell when crushed. This plant can cause convulsions and hallucinations.

(g) Hemlock. Another very poisonous plant.

There were also many satanic artifacts on earth, one of the most dramatic being the "hand of glory." To make this sinister black charm, a hand was cut from the corpse of a hanged man, dried and then prepared to a specific formula. The hand (which could be the left or right) was cut from the body of any criminal left swinging on a roadside gibbet. It was then wrapped in a winding sheet and firmly squeezed absolutely dry, so that no drop of blood could remain inside it. The grisly hand was then placed in an earthenware jar for a period of two weeks. In the jar were salt, long peppers, niter and an unknown substance known as "zimat" or "simort." It was then removed from the jar and either exposed to the sun or baked in an oven heated by fern and vervain. Then, this extremely unpleasant charm was ready for use.

A candle was often used, which was fixed in the hand as if in a holder. At other times the hand would become its own macabre candle, with the outstretched fingers and thumb burning merrily for specified lengths of time. The candle also had to be specially prepared and could only be made of virgin wax, the fat of a hanged man and "sisamie de Lapone," which either means Lapland sesame or sesame and horse dung. "Ponie" is the word for horse dung in the dialect of Lower Normandy, where the hand of glory legend is particularly strong.

The charm was often used by witches, but its most positive use belonged to thieves. As long as the fingers or the candle remained alight, then everyone in the household would remain in a charmed sleep while their valuables were removed. If one finger of the hand burned out, it would mean that one member of the household was still up and about.

Any household anxious to protect itself from this form of housebreaking (last reported case was at Loughcrew, County Meath in 1831), was advised to smear all doors with an ointment, the ingredients of which were fairly difficult to come by—the fat of a white hen, the gall of a black cat and the blood of a screech owl.

Jinxing has always been a great satanic weapon, based on the idea that man can only accept so much from coincidence. For instance, there was the case of the German battleship *Scharnhorst*, which, when only half complete, rolled on its side, killing sixty workmen. At its official launching in October 1936, Hitler and Goering arrived to find that the ship had somehow launched itself the previous night and had severely damaged a number of barges. During its first piece of action a gun on the *Scharnhorst*'s deck exploded, killing nine men. Later its air supply system broke down, suffocating twelve gunners. A year later, badly damaged and under tow, the battleship hit the ocean liner *Bremen*, which was afterward bombarded by the British after it became hopelessly stuck in river mud. Later still, the *Scharnhorst*, under British bombardment, was finally mortally wounded, and sank, taking with her most of her crew. But even her survivors were not to go unscathed—and two were later found on a beach, killed by the emergency oil heater that exploded when they tried to light it.

Earlier there was the sinister case of the car belonging to the Archduke Ferdinand, victim of the famous 1914 assassination. Soon after the start of the First World War, the car came into the possession of General Potiorek of the Austrian army, who was later defeated, disgraced and died insane. The next owner, an Austrian captain on Potiorek's staff, was killed in a motor accident nine days after taking possession of the vehicle. The jinx was nulled until the end of the war, when the next owner, the Governor of Yugoslavia, had four accidents in four months in the car. He hurriedly sold the rogue vehicle to a doctor who, six months later, was found crushed with the car on top of him. The next owner was a jeweler who committed suicide after owning it for a year, the next a racing driver who was killed in it, and the ninth victim was a Serbian farmer who died when the car overturned. The tenth and final victim was a garage owner who was killed, along with four others, when the car was involved in yet another accident. The jinxed vehicle is now in a Viennese museum. So far the museum and its staff are intact.

Another car which had a dark history was the Porsche sports car in which the movie star James Dean was killed. Repaired after his death, many other owners were involved in disastrous accidents in it.

A plane was also involved in a jinx situation—a Lockheed Constellation which suffered a number of bizarre

misfortunes between 1945 and 1949. In July 1945 a me-
chanic walked into one of the propellers and was killed
instantly. A year later a pilot died of heart failure at the
controls. In 1947 a new engine caught fire and almost
killed everybody. After a year of peace, the final denoue-
ment came on July 10, 1949, when the Constellation
crashed near Chicago, killing all passengers and crew.

One of the most spectacular jinxes was on the *Great
Eastern*, Brunel's famous ship. Brunel died from a heart
attack on her deck shortly after the *Great Eastern's* com-
pletion, a riveter and an apprentice vanished without
trace during her construction, on her maiden voyage five
men were scalded to death when a closed steam escape
valve caused an explosion, and during the rest of her life
the tragedies and disasters were too numerous to document here. Fifteen years after her launching, the acci-
dent-prone *Great Eastern* was towed into Milford Haven
where she rusted up and blocked the shipping lanes.
Breaking up the enormous hulk had to be done with a
huge iron ball. The final venomous shock was to come.
Inexplicably, inside the iron ball were found the skele-
tons of the riveter and the boy. A final satanic trick to
end the career of that great demonic ship.

The final sphere of satanic influence on earth are satanic domains. These are largely traditional—bridges, natural chasms, dikes, ravines and stagnant pools. The legendary inexplicable always happens in these areas. But
certainly the most dramatic of all these domains are the
"Devil's graveyards." One such mysterious graveyard is
sited in the Sargasso Sea. Some years after the Second
World War, two British airliners mysteriously vanished,
and an intensive search revealed nothing. This area is
part of the notorious Bermuda Triangle, and since 1945
over a hundred ships and aircraft have disappeared without trace in the vicinity. No bodies or wreckage have ever

been found. But there are records of disappearances in the Triangle since 1609, and they are still taking place. One typical disappearance was a USAF Boeing Stratotanker which had taken off from Langley in Virginia and was heading toward the Azores. Just after takeoff very weak radio signals, which eventually faded away, were heard from the plane. A widespread search revealed nothing. However, there have been some narrow misses and as a result there are some very strange survivors' stories. Captain Dan Henry was aboard a tug towing an empty nitrate barge through the area in 1966 in calm and clear weather. Suddenly the sea became rough, a thick fog descended, the compass began to swing and all electrical power failed. Captain Henry signaled full speed ahead and after a struggle pulled free.

A couple of years earlier, in 1964, pilot Chuck Wakely recorded another narrow miss in the Devil's graveyard of the Bermuda Triangle. He was on a solo flight from Nassau to Miami, climbing to about 8,000 ft. When he had leveled off, Wakely noticed a faint glow on the wings of the plane. Five minutes later the glow increased so that he found it difficult to read his instruments. Then all the electronic equipment died, and Wakely was forced to operate the plane manually. The wings also glowed and seemed to have no clear outline. Eventually, after the glow became unbearably blinding, it began slowly to fade away.

In 1963 the crew of a Boeing 707 noticed what appeared to be an atomic explosion within the Triangle. They checked with the coastguard and were told that no disturbance had been reported. So the main overall mystery is why all electrical power seems to have vanished in the surviving planes and ships. The compass disorientation could be explained by a large iron deposit under the seabed. But there are other inexplicable happenings, such as the glow, the fog, the tumultuous sea and the explosion.

An area in the Pacific, 800 miles SE of Japan, between Iwo Jima and Marcus Island is known as the Devil's sea. Similar occurences have been reported there. For instance, between 1950 and 1954 nine ships disappeared there without a trace. One possible explanation, put forward by Ivan Sanderson, the naturalist and writer, is that both the Bermuda Triangle and the Devil's Sea are almost in the same latitude—between 30° and 40° north of the Equator. But these are not the only Devil's graveyards and there are reported to be twelve such areas. The Bermuda Triangle is the best-known only because it lies in one of the world's busiest shipping lanes. Two of these areas are sited on land, one in the Sahara and the other in the mountains of northwest India. Sanderson's theory is that the majority of the Devil's graveyards lie in sections of the ocean where warm and cold currents collide and that these sections are "nodal points" where surface and subsurface currents go in different directions. He argues that the powerful movements of these subsurface currents cause magnetic vortices. But this does not really explain the strange condition of sea and air—and the termination of all electricity. Also, a number of ships have been found abandoned in these ocean areas, the crews having disappeared. Why did they leave their ships? What did they see?

The Devil's Dike, the Devil's Chair, Devil's Water, Devil's Canyon—all are duplicated everywhere in the Christian and non-Christian world. Dark tracts of countryside, still water and strange geological shapes all have caught the public imagination—and associated them with satanic influence. The most vivid description of such contaminated ground appears in H. P. Lovecraft's evocative short story, "The Dunwich Horror":

. . . he comes upon a lonely and curious country. The ground gets higher, and the briar-bordered stone walls press closer and closer against the ruts of the dusty, curving road. The trees of the frequent forest belts seem too large and the wild weeds, brambles and grasses attain a luxuriance not often found. . . . Gorges and ravines of problematic depth intersect the way, and the crude wooden bridges always seem of dubious safety. When the road dips again there are stretches of marshland that one instinctively dislikes, and indeed almost fears at evening when unseen whippoorwills chatter and the fireflies come out in abnormal profusion to dance to the raucous, creepily insistent rhythms of stridently piping bullfrogs.

Everyone has his own idea of hell on earth, and indeed Satan's dominion is a mixture of unexplained fact, fear and fantasy. But this in no way renders it powerless—if anything it makes it more awesome. But it is not so much Satan's outposts, artifacts and servants that are really responsible for strengthening the powers of evil—it is the satanists themselves.

Satanists are those who worship Satan in a practical manner. One modern definition comes from an American group of satanists—the Our Lady of Endor Coven of the Ophite Cultus Sathanas. Their philosophy of satanism is "the position opposed to the force that brought the cosmos into existence." Its credo is "the realization that the universe is negative to man." But the worship of Satan began at the very root of Christianity. The Gnostic sects were the first to practice a form of satanism. To the Gnostics, the world about them was a deeply evil place— indeed, they saw the world itself as hell and their lives on it nothing short of a prison sentence. The God of the Jews was seen as the great evil power ruling on earth, and the entire Old Testament was, to the Gnostics, a complete renunciation of Christian values. No God could be good who created such a wicked world. In their view the real God was a remote one, living in some distant heaven whilst the evil Yahwek ruled the world.

Jesus was seen by the Gnostics as the potential Savior, the son of the distant God. The Old Testament became a document of tyranny, with the prophets and servants of the evil God Yahwek becoming the villains of the piece—and the original villains such as Esau, Cain and the Sodomites becoming heroes. The serpent in the Garden of Eden, for instance, was seen by the Gnostics as a messenger from the distant God, intent on giving Adam and Eve the knowledge of good and evil so that they would understand how evil Yahwek's creation of the world was. Some Gnostics, however, refused to accept Christ at all, claiming that he was not the son of the distant God but the son of Yahwek and was therefore up to no good.

As the Ten Commandments were also obviously evil, the Gnostics were split in their approach to living in a hell on earth. Some chose to break every moral rule and live as self-indulgently as possible. Others chose to keep themselves immune from contamination by living lives of total self-denial. Rather more conveniently, another group of Gnostics believed that once they had received the gnosis, i.e., the true knowledge of Yahwek's evil rule—then complete self-indulgence could be had without fear of moral pollution. St. Irenaeus, writing censoriously in the second century, claimed that this group believed the only way they could liberate themselves from Yahwek's clutches was to run the full gamut of human experience. They did "all those things which we dare not

63

either speak or hear of, nay which we must not even conceive in our thoughts."

A. E. Housman in his *Last Poems* said:

> We for a certainty are not the first
> Have sat in taverns while the tempest hurled
> Their hopeful plans to emptiness, and cursed
> Whatever brute and blackguard made the world.

The basic inability of man to accept the exigencies of a hard world and its temptations can be seen in the continuing Gnostic influence, which was eventually taken into Western Europe by way of the Bogomils and Cathars. The Bogomils, active in Bulgaria in the tenth century, also believed that the Old Testament God was Satan. However, they elaborated on this theme by claiming that the good, distant God had two sons, Satanel and Michael. Satanel rebelled and was ejected from heaven whilst Michael remained. Satanel, once on earth, created Adam's body but he lacked the power to give him life. By cunning, Satanel persuaded God to breathe life into Adam. Then, having succeeded in this confidence trick, he taught Adam how to corrupt the coming race of mankind. Satanel seduced Eve, and became the evil God of the Jews. Eventually Michael, as Jesus, came to earth in a desperate bid to unseat his brother, but Satanel had him crucified. But as a result of this great act of wickedness, Satanel lost his overall power as well as the last two letters of his name, which meant God. Thus the more familiar limited but seductive tempter, Satan, emerged.

Bogomil missionaries brought the substance of this belief to the Cathars in the south of France, and during the early thirteenth century an armed crusade was sent against them, so strong had the cult become. Basically the Cathar belief was that the world had been created by an evil God whose name was either Yahwek or Satan. The body was a prison to the spirit and the Christian Church was an autocracy, founded to enslave mankind. Cathars were strongly against marriage and procreation (more souls to be imprisoned by Satan) and they refused to have anything to do with Christian sacraments. Rather like the Gnostics, the Cathars either remained aloof from the world in contained self-discipline or were as lustful as possible so as to avoid marriage and producing more souls for enslavement. Presumably the illegitimate children they produced were considered less sinful than those born in wedlock. The Cathars' main scorn was directed toward the Roman Catholic Church, an institution which they considered totally evil and corrupt. In its turn the Church branded the Cathars as satanists— which is exactly how the Cathars branded the Church

Throughout the ensuing centuries a number of groups were labeled as satanists by the Church, and accusations were made against the Albigensians, Waldensians, the Knights Templar and the Brethren of the Cross, as well as individuals like Dr. John Dee and Edward Kelley.

Despite the fact that this book is mainly concerned with more recent satanic activities, Sir Francis Dashwood's Hell-Fire Club is worth discussing briefly, mainly because its philosophy of *"Fais Ce Que Voudras"*, "Do What Thou Wilt," was also to become the philosophy of later Devil worshipers. Dashwood owned a large estate in West Wycombe, Buckinghamshire, in the eighteenth century, and had also married a rich widow. In the mid-eighteenth century, satire and caricature were very much the fashion, and Dashwood's friend and manipulator, Paul Whitehead, was a decadent and originally bankrupt figure with a taste for the vicarious. Together they had taken "grand tours" around the more erotic archeological discoveries in Europe as well as the arousing private rooms of the Cardinal in the Vatican. They had also acquired various handbooks of spells including various Grimoires (see later chapters). When the impressionable Dashwood arrived in Italy, the country was on the crest of a revival of interest in the black arts. Also the eroticism of Greek, Roman, Turkish and Indian art had a very strong effect on the unliberated passions of a man who had been used to English puritanism.

At the same time, in England, there had been another revival of interest, not so much in the black arts, but in rather esoteric or alternatively merely crude satanic clubs. Lord Wharton, for instance, had founded the original Hell-Fire Club, which met for the explicit purposes of "drinking, gambling and blaspheming." Such clubs spread very quickly, largely among the aristocracy, and became so notorious that a Royal Proclamation banned them in 1721. This only made them more stimulating to their members, and underground organizations such as the Edinburgh Sweating Club, the Dublin Blasters and the Demoniacs flourished.

Dashwood, Whitehead and other aristocratic aesthetes began to meet at a pub in Cornhill named The George and Vulture. This was the original meeting place of the first Hell-Fire Club and, at first, the group was heavily influenced by Rosicrucianism.* Later the group, known as The Secret Brotherhood, the Order of the Friars of Saint Francis of Wycombe, began to meet at Medmenham Abbey—a derelict twelfth-century Cistercian monastery he had leased. Hugh Walpole met Dashwood on his grand tour and there witnessed the following satanic

*A secret society devoted to occult studies founded by Christian Rosenkreuz.

The Rosicrucian Society did not exist as an organized body until the nineteenth century. There are now four organized sects of Rosicrucians in the United States.

rite—the kind of occasion that Dashwood would regularly attend. Walpole described the scene in his book *Mem-
oirs of the Reign of King George III.*

On Good Friday, each person who attends the Sis-
tine Chapel takes a small scourge from an attendant
at the door. The chapel is dimly lighted, only three
candles, which are extinguished by the priest, one by
one. At the putting out of the first, the penitents take
off one part of their dress. At the next, still more, and
in the dark which follows the extinguishing of the
third candle, "lay on" their own shoulders with
groans and lamentations. Sir Francis Dashwood,
thinking this mere stage effect, entered with the others dressed in a large watchman's coat, demurely
took his scourge from the priest and advanced to the
end of the chapel, where in the darkness ensuing he
drew from beneath his coat an English horsewhip
and flogged right and left quite down the Chapel—
the congregation exclaiming "II Diavolo! II Diavolo!"—thinking the evil one was upon them with a
vengeance. The consequence might have been serious had Dashwood not immediately fled the Papal
dominions.

Dashwood's "Order" lasted for some thirty-five years
and although it was not a group-conceived joke, it was
definitely far more harmless than activities two centuries later. Dashwood liked to bring his fantasies to life,
however, not only in the Medmenham Abbey but also in
the caves he constructed nearby. He considerably refurb-
ished the sinister abbey, adding an artificial gothic tower
and frescoes on walls and ceiling. Voluptuous statues
were another addition and a pleasure boat was provided
so that the "monks" could cruise up and down the

Thames, bent on one nefarious pleasure or the other. Meanwhile the abbey church was restored into a common room with a pagan altar. The figure of the Virgin and Child was removed from the church and placed in the new tower. But many of the artifacts and statues around the building were classically sexual as well as satanic. Walpole wrote:

> This Abbey is now become remarkable by being hired by a set of gentlemen who have erected themselves into a sort of fraternity of monks and pass two days in each month there. Each has his own cell into which they may carry women. They have a maid to dress their dinner and no other servants.

The caves themselves run down from a 200-foot entrance, into the center of the hill. Various recesses had been cut out, one of which may have served as a robing room. Roman numerals were cut out in the white chalk but their meaning is obscure. They read XXII—F and a village rhyme gives only a clue to their meaning:

> Take twenty steps and rest awhile
> Then take a pick and find the style
> Where once I did my love beguile
> 'twas twenty-two in Dashwood's time
> Perhaps to hid this cell divine
> Where lay my love in peace sublime.

There is also the legend of a secret passage and the rumor of a girl nicknamed St. Agnes who served the monks as a vestal virgin and lived in a secret chamber.

A labyrinth leads out of the tunnel, and this was laid out to the exact design of the Tantric * "fertilized world-

---

* Tantra is an Indian cult of ecstasy.

egg." This meant that it was bisected twice and once through the center. There were other designs in the caves to link in with Tantra. About 300 feet below the top of the hill, and on a level with the floor of the valley, flowed an underground river which Sir Francis Dashwood named the River Styx. Past the river was the Inner Temple where two symbols were recently found carved into the wall. The first was a bas-relief key measuring about 5½ inches. The other was an ovoid representation of a vulva.

There is no really clear indication as to the exact nature of Dashwood's cult but it would appear to be partly Tantric, partly the pursuit of sexual magic and energy—and partly satanic.

Perhaps the most curious and most misunderstood of more contemporary satanists is Aleister Crowley. Branded "the Wickedest Man in the World" by the popular press, Crowley was, in fact, a strange combination of aesthete, manipulator, sexual and real-life adventurer, power seeker, dominator and snob. He was incapable of compassion and his love was largely for himself. But there is no doubt that he was a major satanic figure in that he was able to dominate completely other people's minds. So successful was he in this that he could conjure up alien emotion, visions and hallucinatory tricks, making his victims believe that they were in the grip of diabolical possession.

Cagliostro, Sir Edward Kelley, the Comte de Saint-Germain, Eliphas Levi and Madama Blavatsky were Crowley's magical forebears, and indeed he often claimed that he was the reincarnation of Levi—among other past lives. Crowley saw his task as bringing Oriental wisdom to Europe and at the same time restoring paganism in a puristic form. He was aware of the fractured nature of his personality as this letter to Jacintha Buddicom indicates. It was written in the last year of his life, 1947:

I had at that time a little rose and cross—five rubies and a five-petal rose with a cross of six squared with various inscriptions, and I arranged with myself that when I put this on I should act in one character, and when I took it off again in another. This was a great help to me in sorting out the various elements of my being. It was not a matter of the magical personality so much, I simply built up two people of entirely different characteristics. One, for example, might be a scholar, a mountaineer, and explorer—a person of great athletic achievements, generous in disposition, noble, and so on. The other character had a whole lot of other characteristics, very distinct from those of the first, and I used to punish myself if, when I was one character, I performed any action which was suited only to the other.

In many but totally opposite ways Crowley emulated his father. Edward Crowley was a brewer but his obsession lay with the Plymouth Brethren, of which he was a very active member. Crowley Senior spent much of his time traveling up and down the country preaching and trying to gain converts. Aleister was brought up firmly within this teaching and he soon grew to hate its narrow, puritanical standpoint. He also became a Plymouth Brother and for a while he was satisfied. As his biographer, John Symonds, writes:

In his childish ardour, he thought of himself as a Christian knight, doing deeds of holiness and valour; he wanted to excel himself for Christ, as he excelled himself, when he grew up, for Ra-Hoor-Khuit, the Egyptian god of war, in the religion of his own making.

70

By eleven Crowley's father was dead and the devout son was finding himself more and more aroused by descriptions of torture. He enjoyed in his imaginaton suffering at the hands of violent, whorish women. He found certain parts of Revelations very much to his liking, particularly the False Prophet, the Great Beast and the Scarlet Woman. Later his mother was to call him the Great Beast and it is possible that he genuinely believed himself to be the Antichrist. He was expelled from a Plymouth Brethren School for "corrupting" another boy and continued with his hated education at Malvern, Tonbridge and later at Oxford. Crowley's mother was also deeply religious—and apparently unsympathetic to the unlikable but understandable mess she and her husband had made of their son. The feeling was mutual, for Crowley hated his mother, calling her "a brainless bigot of the most narrow, logical and inhuman type."

Crowley's background made him hate the Christian religion with utter venom, and he clearly decided, like the Gnostics centuries before him, that hell was on earth and administered by God. He then took the clear and conscious decision to worship the other side—and to re-create the old paganism in a variety of colorful ways. Some were ludicrous, others eccentric and the more minor clearly revolting. There is considerable proof of his sadism and isolationism throughout his life, but a disturbing example of it occurred at a very early stage. Trying to prove whether a cat had nine lives or not, Crowley writes:

> I caught a cat, and having administered a large dose of arsenic, I chloroformed it, hanged it above the gas jet, stabbed it, cut its throat, smashed its skull, and, when it had been pretty throughly burnt,

drowned it and threw it out of the window that the fall might remove the ninth life. The operation was successful. I was genuinely sorry for the animal; I simply forced myself to carry out the experiment in the interests of pure science.

Crowley's happiest and purest moments were climbing mountains, to which he was addicted. The adventure of it all gave him the same kind of elation as his satanic and was one of his safer activities. Nevertheless he was better off climbing alone, for he was irresistibly drawn to harming whoever accompanied him in any situation. In 1898 Crowley wrote and had privately printed (like most of his works) a long poem called "Aceldama: A Place to Bury Strangers in." One of the verses illustrates his growing state of mind:

> All degradation, all sheer infamy,
> Thou shalt endure. Thy head beneath the mire
> And dung of worthless women shall desire
> As in some hateful dream, at last to lie;
> Woman must trample thee till thou respire that
>   deadliest fume;
> The vilest worms must crawl, the loathliest
>   vampires gloom.

Crowley wanted to suffer as a result of his spiritual defection but he also wanted to make others suffer too. A number of other erotic and demonic works followed Aceldama, such as *The Tale of Archais, Songs of the Spirit, The Poem, Jezebel, Jephthah and White Stains*, which were all published in the same year, financed by Crowley's sizable but rapidly dwindling private fortune.

In 1898 Crowley was introduced into the Hermetic Order of the Golden Dawn, which was dominated by Mac-

Gregor Mathers. Instantly Crowley became more magically ambitious and took the title Perdurabo (I will endure to the end). The Golden Dawn had a membership of about a hundred and included such teachings as how to create magic circles, consecrate talismans, use magic weapons, travel astrally and understand the Cabbala. The society disapproved of magic emanating from drugs or sex and concentrated solely on ceremonial magic. This policy was to continually frustrate Crowley, who at that time was living in London under the name of Count Svareff, a Russian nobleman. This artificial disguise was one of the many pseudonyms that Crowley invented and each pseudonym invariably had to be of noble rank. Never did Crowley descend to working class identities.

It was only a matter of time before Crowley was to quarrel with Mathers, or Samuel Liddell Mathers as he was known. But for the moment he held an uneasy truce with him. Mathers was basically an academic, having translated a number of major works including the *Kabbalah Unveiled, The Key of Solomon* and *The Book of the Sacred Magic of Abra-Melin the Mage.* Crowley was much impressed by the last-mentioned, which involved a yogalike technique in which seclusion and purification were necessary adjuncts. In order to do this, Crowley retired to Boleskine House, near Foyers in Inverness. The Russian title was dropped and a new one invented—that of Lord or the Laird of Boleskine. Needless to say Crowley had not one drop of Scottish blood in him.

Yeats best sums up the growing antagonism of The Golden Dawn to Crowley and why they had refused to let the Laird of Boleskine into the Second Order in a letter to Lady Gregory dated 25th April 1900. He wearily confides:

I have had a bad time of it lately. I told you I was putting MacGregor out of the Kabbala [the Order].

73

Well, last week, he sent a mad person whom we had refused to initiate—to take possession of the rooms and on being ejected attempted to retake possession. . . . Having failed in this he has taken out a summons on the ground that he is "Mathers's envoy," and that there is nothing in the constitution of the Society to enable us to depose Mathers. The envoy is really one Crowley, a quite unspeakable person. He is I believe seeking vengeance for our refusal to initiate him. We did not admit him because we did not think a mystical society was intended to be a reformatory.

Crowley needed experiences—and the more vivid the better. Only this form of stimulation could produce his "aura." His main experiences involved mountain climbing and women. Both extracted from him the full force of his personality. Mountains drew him because of their mysticism and physical dangers. Women drew him because of his ability both to dominate and sexually excite them. Although there were homosexual episodes in Crowley's life, these seemed to be mere concessions to partaking of all the aspects of his philosophy and teaching. In all probability Crowley was heterosexual. He did, however, like some of his women as primitive as possible. The kind of whores he picked up are encapsulated in this idealistic (to Crowley) picture of one of them. He liked "the insatiable intensity of passion that blazed from her evil inscrutable eyes, and tortured her worn face into a whirlpool of seductive sin."

Restlessly, Crowley traveled around the globe. He went to Mexico and later to Ceylon. In 1903 Crowley was twenty-eight and had married Sir Gerald Kelly's sister—Rose, a neurotic and highly impressionable girl. Her family were appalled, instinctively realizing that Rose had damned herself to a fate that was inexorable.

On the way back from Ceylon, Crowley stopped off in Cairo and assumed yet another exotic identity. This time he posed as Prince Chioa Khan and the wretched Rose became Princess Khan. He insisted that everyone address them in these roles—even Rose's parents. Unfortunately Rose's mother, unable to be entirely tactful about her son-in-law's new title, addressed a letter to the couple with an exclamation mark. Angrily, Crowley sent it back unopened.

But despite his fantasies, Crowley was beginning to find life as purposeless as it was financially unrewarding, for his fortune was running out fast, and his debts were mounting. The desperation grew so intense that a revelation came to him and reassured him of his power. In other words, Crowley's frustrated but aspiring mind asserted itself just in time. Aiwaz, Crowley's adopted Holy Guardian Angel, appeared to him in his Cairo flat, and with both ease and efficiency dictated an hour's message to mankind. Crowley took this down with delight and the next day Aiwaz returned for another session, reassuring Crowley that he was "a messenger from the forces ruling this earth at present." Aiwaz returned a third time, and when he left, Crowley had taken down three chapters of the Book of the Law. Not only was this angelically (or demonically) delivered tome a future basis for Crowley's satanic philosophy, but his most famous phrase emerged—"Do What Thou Wilt Shall Be the Whole of The Law." Here is a typical extract from Aiwaz's "dictation":

We have nothing with the outcast and the unfit: let them die in their misery. For they feel not. Compassion is the vice of kings: stamp down the wretched & the weak: this is the law of the strong: this is our law and the joy of the world. Think not, O king, upon that lie: That Thou Must Die; verily thou shalt not die, but live. Now let it be understood: If the body of the King dissolve, he shall remain pure ecstasy for ever. Nuit! Hadit! Ra-Hoor-Khuit! The Sun, Strength & Sight, Light; these are for the servants of the Star and the Snake.

Crowley stole a glance at his satanic visitor and described him as being suspended in a cloudlike substance. He "seemed to be a tall, dark man in his thirties, well knit, active and strong, with the face of a savage king, and eyes veiled lest their gaze should destroy what they saw."

The Book of The Law is written in distinctive Crowley style, Aiwaz or not, and is full of archetype phrases. Here are a selection:

To worship me take wine and strange drugs whereof I will tell my prophet, & be drunk thereof.

There is no law beyond Do what thou wilt.

Be strong, O man! lust, enjoy all things of sense and rapture: fear not that any God shall deny thee for this.

Now ye shall know that the chosen priest and apostle of infinite space is the price-priest the Beast.

If Crowley is to be believed, a strange coincidence had originally made him aware of a coming revelation. Pregnant and slightly dazed, Rose had kept telling Crowley that "they are waiting for you." A little later she suddenly said, "He who was waiting was Horus." Apparently

Crowley had offended this Egyptian god and an apology was due. But what was most surprising was that Rose knew absolutely nothing about Egyptology and certainly nothing about Horus, including the name itself. She then led Crowley into the Boulak Museum (now the National Museum) and without pausing took him past several statues of Horus. Then, upstairs, she stopped at an image of Horus as the hawk-headed Ra-Hoor-Khuit. It was painted upon a wooden stele of the twenty-sixth dynasty. But this was not the point. It was the exhibit number that Crowley claims horrified him. The image's display number was 666—the number of the Great Beast of the Revelations. The Great Beast that Crowley claimed to be.

Horus was vitally important to the Book of The Law. Its cosmology involved two aeons which occurred in the history of the world. In the first aeon, Isis, women dominated the world as a matriarchy. In the second aeon, Osiris, men dominated the world as a patriarchy. This was also the time of the Christian period as well as that of Judaism, Mohammedanism and Buddhism. In 1904 a third aeon arrived—that of Horus the child. But Horus, in Crowley's own interpretation, was a demonic child, for he represented the will, or true-self, of man as opposed to the outside authority, priests and gods.

In 1904 Crowley declared war on Mathers by writing to him, pointing out that the Secret Chiefs had made him the head of the Golden Dawn with a new magical policy—Thelema—will, or true-self. The Secret Chiefs were the mystical governors of the society, and Mathers claimed to have met them in the Bois de Boulogne one night, an encounter in which they gave him his senior post. Crowley, however, claimed that Mathers had merely met an inferior group of demons while *he* had conversed and taken instruction from the mystical pagan deities themselves.

77

Crowley wrote:

> The first important result of the new revelation was the information from the Secret Chiefs that the New Aeon implied the breaking up of the civilisation existing at the time. The nature of Horus being "Force and Fire," his Aeon should be marked by the collapse of humanitarianism. The first act of His reign would naturally be to plunge the world into the catastrophe of a huge and ruthless war.

Mathers eventually responded and launched several "magical attacks" on Crowley, none of which seemed to be very effective. Crowley responded by drawing on the forty-nine servants of Beelzebub. One was Nimorup, "a stunted dwarf with large head and ears. His lips are greeny-bronze and slobbery." Another was Nominon, "A large red spongy jellyfish with one greenish luminous spot, like a nasty mess." If the other forty-seven were anything like these two, then they were awesome indeed!

Crowley's imagination was highly developed and some of his poetry was interesting—even uplifting. But a good deal of it is merely childishly obscene. A typical example is the ludicrous poem "Rosa Mystica." Headed "To pe or not to pe," a part of this downbeat parody of Hamlet's soliloquy reads:

> To pe or not to pe: that is the question:
> Whether 'tis nobler in the mind to suffer
> the slings and arrows of outrageous stricture
> Or to take arms against a close urethra
> And by abscission, end it? To fuck; to come:
> No more; and, by a come to say we end
> The cockstand and the thousand natural lusts

That flesh is heir to. 'Tis a consummation
Devoutly to be wished. To fuck: to come:
To come, perchance to clap! Ay, there's the rub.
For from that come of fuck what clap
may catch . . .

and so on. Compare this with the much more interesting

O for a lily-white goat,
Crisp as a thicket of thorns
With a collar of gold for its throat,
And a scarlet bow for its horns.

Or

Kill off mankind,
And give the earth a chance;
Nature may find
In her Inheritance
Some seedlings of a race
Less infinitely base . . .

The next year saw a disastrous mountain climbing
expedition in which Crowley furthered his gathering evil
reputation by beating porters and by deserting avalanche
buried companions. In 1910 he published *The Scented
Garden of Abdullah the Satirist of Shiraz*, a phony trans-
lation from the nonexistent Persian of some erotic homosexual love poems. He then founded his own magical society, called the Argenteum Astrum—the Silver Star.
This was meant to constitute the Inner Order of The
Great White Brotherhood. The outer order he claimed to
be the Golden Dawn. In other words, because he had
been forbidden to enter the Second Order of the Golden
Dawn, Crowley had merely created his own—cheerfully

"taking over" the Golden Dawn's name at the same time.

With the formation of the new society, Crowley brought out his own propaganda magazine, *The Equinox*. By the time he was thirty Crowley's desire for positive satanism was as strong as ever and he wrote to his brother-in-law, Gerald Kelly:

> After five years of folly and weakness, miscalled politeness, tact, discretion, care for the feeling of others, I am weary of it. I say today; to hell with Christianity, Rationalism, Buddhism, all the lumber of the centuries. I bring you a positive and primaeval fact, Magic by name; and with this I will build me a new Heaven and a new Earth. I want none of your faint approval or faint dispraise; I want blasphemy, murder, rape, revolution, anything, bad or good, but strong.

Gerald Kelly's reaction must have been strong, too, particularly as Rose had a young child and was trekking over China with a husband who scarcely cared for her and who had grown tired of their encumbrance. Crowley confides this by writing, "I found myself in the middle of China with a wife and child. I was no longer influenced by love for them, no longer interested in protecting them as I had been."

Crowley returned to Liverpool in 1906 where he was genuinely shocked to hear that his daughter had died. He felt no remorse at leaving mother and child, merely recording that "she had neglected to cleanse the nipple of the feeding bottle, and thereby exposed the child to the germs of typhoid."

The meetings of the A. A. Society were held at 124 Victoria Street in London and it was here that Crowley claims Satan joined one of their ceremonies.

On one occasion the God came to us in human form (we were working in a locked temple) and remained with us, perfectly perceptible to all our senses, for the best part of an hour, only vanishing when we were physically exhausted by the ecstasy of intimate contact with His divine person. We sank into a sort of sublime stupor; when we came to ourselves, He was gone. Again, at Victoria Street, a number of us were dancing round the altar with linked hands and faces turned outwards. The temple was dimly lighted and thick with incense. Somehow the circle was broken, and we kept on dancing, each for himself. Then we became aware of the presence of a stranger. Some of us counted the men present, and found there was one too many. One of the weaker brethren got scared, or one of the stronger brethren remembered his duty to science—I don't know which—and switched on the light. No stranger was to be seen.

Meanwhile Rose, although having dutifully borne Crowley another child, was falling more and more out of favor as is reflected by this poem:

Rose of the World!
If so, then what a world!
What worm at its red heart lay curled
from the beginning? Plucked and torn and trampled
And utterly corrupt is she . . .

In the autumn of 1911 Rose's nerves finally snapped

and to the horror of her family, the fate they had predicted caught up with her—Crowley divorced her and, suffering from alcoholism, she entered a mental hospital.

Crowley's doubtful fame was spreading and in 1912 he was visited by Theodor Reuss, a German Freemason of some note. Reuss accused Crowley of giving away magical secrets. He quoted from another book of Crowley's, *Liber CCCXXXIII: The Book of Lies*, in which Crowley said, "Let the adept be armed with his Magick Rood and provided with his Mystic Rose." In other words the German Freemason was accusing him of unleashing the secret that sex can be used either magically or ritually. Reuss belonged to the Order of the Templars of the East, which felt itself to be the sole guardian of the secret, and it could communicate in nine degrees the secrets of the Illuminati, the Rosicrucians, the Order of the Hidden Church of the Holy Grail, the Knights of the Holy Ghost, and the Knights of St. John, of Malta and of the Holy Sepulchre. The Order of the Templars of the East declared that:

> Our order possesses the KEY which opens up all masonic and Hermetic secrets, namely, the teaching of *sexual magic*, and this teaching explains, without exception, all the secrets of Nature, all the *symbolism* of FREEMASONRY and all systems of religion.

Later Crowley was made Head of the British Order of the Society, presumably on the basis of "if you can't beat 'em, join 'em." At a ceremony in Berlin he was given the title of "the Supreme and Holy King of Ireland, Iona, and all the Britains that are in the Sanctuary of the Gnosis."

At the beginning of the First World War, Crowley went to America. A *World Magazine* journalist celebrated his arrival with a long report of Crowley's London activities:

I found myself in a large, high-ceilinged studio the atmosphere of which was coloured a deep blue by the reek of a peculiar smelling incense. In the first room stood row on row of books bound in black and marked on their backs with queer, malformed crosses wrought in silver. The second room was fitted up with divans and literally carpeted with multitudes of cushions tossed here and yon. In the third and largest room stood a tall perpendicular canopy under which the high priest sat during the celebration of black mass. Directly in front of it, on a floor tesselated and mosaiced with parti-colored patterns and marked with cabbalistic signs, stood the altar, a black pedestal on top of which was affixed a golden circle. Across the latter lay a golden serpent, as if arrested in the act of crawling. I heard someone behind a curtain playing a weird Chinese-like air on some sort of stringed instrument.

The feel of the whole place was decidedly uncanny. . . . One by one the worshippers entered. They were mostly women of aristocratic type. Their delicate fingers adorned with costly rings, their rustling silks, the indefinable elegance of their carriage attested their station in life. It was whispered to me that not a few people of noble descent belonged to the Satanists. Everybody wore a little black domino which concealed the upper part of the face, making identification impossible. Hung with black velvet curtains, the place presented a decidedly sepulchral aspect. The complexions of the women seemed as white as wax. There was a fitful light furnished by a single candlestick having seven branches. Suddenly this went out and the place was filled with subterranean noises like the sound of a violent wind moving among innumerable leaves. Then came the slow, monotonous chant of the high priest: "There is no good. Evil is good. Blessed be the Principle of Evil. All hail, Prince of the World, to whom even God Himself has given dominion." A sound of evil bleating filled the pauses of these blasphemous utterances. . . .

Throughout this period in America, Crowley continued to practice his "sexual magic" and at the same time waged a strange and rather childish pro-German propaganda campaign. His writing included such jottings, with reference to the bombing, as:

A great deal of damage was done at Croydon, especially at its suburb Addiscombe, where my aunt lives. Unfortunately her house was not hit. Count Zeppelin is respectfully requested to try again. The exact address is Eton Lodge, Outram Road.

Crowley claimed that he was, in fact, helping the Allies and trying "to wreck the German propaganda on the roof of Reductio ad Absurdum." He also grandly stated that his advice to the Germans had been to wage unrestricted submarine warfare which, indirectly, brought the Americans into the war arena. For these services to Britain he reckoned he should be awarded the Victoria Cross. No one, however, was in a rush to give it to him.

During the American period, Crowley took up painting and the following advertisement is typical of the state of his mind.

WANTED

Dwarfs, Hunchbacks, Tattooed Women, Harrison Fisher Girls, Freaks of All Sorts, Coloured Women, only if exceptionally ugly or deformed, to pose for artist. Apply by letter with a photograph.

In America, Crowley rose higher (or promoted himself) in the echelons of satanism. He was now ready to receive the throne itself and proclaim his basic philosophy, i.e., Thelema or "do what thou wilt." This, in his view, would usher in the new age of liberty and end the age of suffering that he considered was caused by the practice of Christianity and other God-worshiping religions. He performed a ceremony to initiate this, at the same time crucifying a frog. The wording ran:

Night being fallen, thou shalt arrest the frog, and accuse him of blasphemy, sedition and so forth, in these words:
Do what thou wilt shall be the whole of the Law. Lo, Jesus of Nazareth, how thou art taken in my snare. All my life long thous hast plagued me and affronted me. In thy name—with all other free souls in Christendom—I have been tortured in my boyhood; all delights have been forbidden unto me; all that I had has been taken from me, and that which is owed to me they pay not—in thy name. Now, at last, I have thee; the Slave-God is in the power of the Lord of Freedom. Thine hour is come; as I blot thee out from this earth, so surely shall the eclipse pass; and Light, Life, Love and Liberty be once more the Law of Earth. Give thous place to me, O, Jesus; thine aeon is

85

passed; the Age of Horus is arisen by the Magick of
the Master the Great Beast.

In 1918 Crowley returned to England and shortly after-
ward set out for Sicily. He took with him his Scarlet
Woman, Leah Hirsig, and his most interesting poem,
"Hymn to Pan," which he wrote in America. Here,
Crowley sees Pan as the Antichrist:

HYMN TO PAN

Thrill with lissome lust of the light,
O man! My man!
Come careering out of the night
Of Pan! Io Pan!
Io Pan! Io Pan! Come over the sea
From Sicily and from Arcady!
Roaming as Bacchus, with fauns and pards
and nymphs and satyrs for thy guards,
On a milk-white ass, come over the sea
To me, to me . . .
I am numb
With the lonely lust of devildom.
Thrust the sword through the galling fetter,
All-devourer, all-begetter;
Give me the sign of the Open Eye,
And the token erect of thorny thigh,
And the word of madness and mystery,
O Pan! Io Pan!
Io Pan! Io Pan Pan! Pan Pan! Pan,
I am a man:
Do as thou wilt, as a great god can,
O Pan! Io Pan!
Io Pan! Io Pan Pan! I am awake
In the grip of the snake,

The eagle slashes with beak and claw;
The gods withdraw:
The great beasts come, Io Pan! I am borne
To death on the horn
of the Unicorn.
I am Pan! Io Pan! Io Pan Pan! Pan!
I am thy mate, I am thy man,
Goat of thy flock, I am gold, I am god,
Flesh to thy bone, flower to thy rod.
With hoofs of steel I race on the rocks
Through solstice stubborn to equinox.
And I rave; and I rape and I rip and I rend
Everlasting, world without end,
Mannikin, maiden, maenad, man,
In the might of Pan,
Io Pan! Io Pan Pan! Pan! Io Pan!

At Cefalu he rented a villa, built up a small community, and created a temple to the new age of Crowley enlightenment within the building. The front door of the villa bore the ominous message DO WHAT THOU WILT. Crowley spent three years in these demonic headquarters studying the occult, Satan-worshiping and further addicting himself to heroin. Just as money was about to run out he received a commission from Collins who published, in 1922, his novel about drug-running called *The Diary of a Drug Fiend.*

Crowley's biographer, John Symonds, draws a vivid portrait of the Great Beast relaxing in his valley, or The Sacred Abbey of Thelema, as he had renamed it.

The spectacle of the Beast, the lobes of his ears pierced and hung with rings, dabbing oil paints on to the canvas, or smoking his opium pipe on the sofa inside the Abbey, ever in the company of two wives, approaches the bourgeois ideal of the respectable, although eccentric, gentleman on holiday.

But Crowley was still able to be objective about himself, and during the abbey period he wrote:

> I am myself a physical coward, but I have exposed myself to every form of disease, accident, and violence; I am dainty and delicate, but I have driven myself to delight in dirty and disgusting debauches, and to devour human excrements and human flesh. I am at this moment defying the power of drugs to disturb my destiny and divert my body from its duty. I am also a mental and moral weakling, whose boyhood training was so horrible that its result was that my will wholly summed up in hatred of all restraint, whose early manhood, untrained, left my mind and animal soul like an elephant in rut broken out of the stockade. Yet I have mastered every mode of my mind, and made myself a morality more severe than any other in the world if only by virture of its absolute freedom from any code of conduct.

On publication of the *Drug Fiend*, the press went to town on Crowley's iniquities, and the *Sunday Express*, predictably enough, led the field. They ran such headlines as:

COMPLETE EXPOSURE OF 'DRUG FIEND' AUTHOR
BLACK RECORD OF ALEISTER CROWLEY. PREYING ON THE DEBASED. HIS ABBEY. PROFLIGACY AND VICE IN SICILY

The article went on to discuss "bestial orgies" in Sicily, "unspeakable orgies, impossible of description."

Crowley was delighted—as were his publishers—and he gained further publicity by writing to Beaverbrook demanding a fair hearing and an independent inquiry. A few months later one of Crowley's disciples, an Oxford undergraduate named Raoul Loveday, wrote a fascinating account of day-to-day domestic life at the abbey with Crowley and his small community:

> The town itself is most lovely, a huddle of high lemon-coloured houses lying between the paws of a titanic rock fashioned roughly like a crouching lion. One of the inhabitants guided us, for it was dusk when we arrived, to the steep hill outside the town on which stands the Abbey. The first thing that we noticed was the words, *Do what thou wilt shall be the whole of the Law*, painted on the main door of the white low house before us. Since this is the password of those within the Abbey, and their invariable greeting, it should be said and understood at once that it upholds not the fulfilment of what one thinks one wants, but of what one ought to think one wants; of the true will.

Loveday went into the temple, which was a large square room out of which five others opened. In the center of a magic circle that was painted on the tiled floor stood a six-sided altar and a Pompeian censer made out of bronze.

Utterly exhausted, Loveday went to bed but was awakened the next morning by the chanting of the watchword of the abbey and the beating of a tomtom. Soon he joined the rest of the community outside on the hill. In unison they stretched out their arms to the sun and began to chant:

> Hail unto Thee who art Ra in Thy rising, even unto Thee who are Ra in Thy strength; who travell-

est over the Heavens in Thy bark at the uprising of the Sun . . . Hail unto Thee from the Abodes of Night.

The remainder of the morning was spent chauvinistically, with shopping, cooking and typing being carried out by the women, while the men apparently wrote down great occult thoughts. At midday they were all voraciously hungry and there was meat, fruit and sharp Sicilian wine. The meal was eaten in silence. The afternoon was considerably more active than the morning. Crowley led some of his disciples in climbing the great rock—a sheer blind buttress near the abbey. Crowley took them up on a rope, and somehow Loveday managed the ascent. At the top was a glorious view of the old town with its Temple of Jupiter and Baths of Diana. High tea followed—and then the ritual of the Pentagram.

The ceremony began with Crowley's disciples intoning, with vibrant intensity, the traditional holy names of God and His archangels at the four cardinal points. The primary object of all this was to enclose themselves in a consecrated square, fortified by the nine names of the archangels. This, they believed, would effectively exclude evil influences. This ritual was then followed by the reading of the Gnostic Collects, which were invocations of a "Higher Force." The aim was to uplift the mind by poetic appeal to the forces of nature, such as the moon. In this case the invocation would be:

Lady of Night that turning ever about us are now visible and now invisible in Thy season, be thou favourable to hunters and lovers, and to all men that toil upon the earth, and to all mariners upon the sea.

The ceremony then ended and talk, chess and mandolin-strumming concluded an energetic day.

The next afternoon was too wet for climbing and so the Black Master proposed a game of "Thelema." Intrigued, Loveday was in for a shock. He followed Crowley to the side of the abbey, where he found a small stone courtyard marked out as if it were a fives court but without side walls. In fact, the resultant game was very similar to rugby fives but was played with an ordinary football. Loveday played an exhausting set with Crowley. Any part of the body was allowed to be used to get the ball up and Loveday found that the game turned out to be more skillful than fives, if less fast. He wrote: ". . . one set fagged us both so that we were glad enough when a break came through the arrival of Hermes and Dionysus."

They were not, however, the gods of those names but two barefoot children of five and six years old. Later, the Great Beast took these two climbing on a nearby pinnacle of rock, and Loveday was amazed at their dexterity and skill. Their small, naked toes fitted into every cranny. Loveday was very impressed and noted that Crowley's philosophy of Do What Thou Wilt had made these two children uninhibited, cool and self-reliant. This was a just observation, but soon these two prodigies were to be deserted by Crowley and left to their own devices.

However, the abbey idyll was not to last. The death of Loveday (from natural causes), Crowley's bizarre funeral service for him, and continuous British press attention finally made the Italian authorities expel him from the abbey—and Italy. The Great Beast, still with his Scarlet Woman, left Cefalu on May 1, 1923.

But Crowley was still at the height of his powers and although his Scarlet Woman and disciples changed as his wandering took him across Europe and North Africa, Crowley remained faithful to his creed of Do What Thou Wilt. The suicide of Norman Mudd, one of his chief minions, furthered Crowley's sinister reputation, and his own continuous desire for new sensation increased his heroin addiction. Meanwhile, the magazine *John Bull* took over the Crowley sensationalism and followed his career with fervid interest, running headlines like A CANNIBAL AT LARGE and THE KING OF DEPRAV-ITY while *Picture Post* also worried away at the Beast's activities with such enticing placards as

THE HUMAN BEAST
NEW DISCOVERIES
EXCLUSIVE

The Mandrake Press published a considerable body of Crowley's work during the thirties, including the famous *Confessions* as well as his magical novel *Moonchild* and some short stories. But the climax of Crowley's public life was to be in the courtroom where he was attempting to sue his old friend Nina Hamnett whose autobiography, published by Constable, made what he considered was a libelous reference to the much missed abbey. The extract from the book, entitled *Laughing Torso* read:

He was supposed to practise Black Magic there, and one day a baby was said to have disappeared mysteriously. There was also a goat there. This all pointed to Black Magic, so people said, and the inhabitants of the village were frightened of him.

Crowley lost the case but some of the dialogue between him and prosecuting counsel Malcolm Hilbery KC, whom Constable had briefed, is well worth reproducing:

Hilbery: (cross-examining Crowley for the Defense) Are you asking for damages because your reputation has suffered?
Crowley: Yes.
H For many years you have been publicly denounced as the worst man in the world?

C Only by the lowest kind of newspaper.

H Did any paper call you "the Monster of Wickedness"?

C I can't remember.

H Have you, from the time of your adolescence, openly defied all moral conventions?

C No.

H And proclaimed your contempt for all the doctrines of Christianity?

C Not all the doctrines . . .

H Did you take to yourself the designation of The Beast 666?

C Yes.

H Do you call yourself The Master Therion?

C Yes.

H What does Therion mean?

C Great Wild Beast.

H Do these titles convey a fair expression of your practice and outlook on life?

C "The Beast 666" only means "sunlight." You can call me "Little Sunshine."

This was followed by laughter in court.

But eventually the barrage of publicity died away and Crowley faded out of public consciousness. Gradually he lost his influence amid a welter of nonprojects such as the proposed opening of a Black Magick Restaurant and the marketing of his Elixir of Life pills—made, in part, of his own semen. He also created, with reasonable success, a course in bodily and sexual rejuvenation. Called Amrita, the course retailed at 25 guineas per weekly session. More writing followed—and considerable correspondence with his followers in America, who still remained loyal, sending him money and goodies through the late thirties right up until the end of the war. On January 17, 1945, he retired to a boarding house in Hastings where his heroin addiction increased, and where loneliness finally caught up with the Great Beast. He died on December 1, 1945, at seventy-two and was cremated at Brighton. A number of his old acolytes were there, and the "Hymn to Pan" was read aloud over the coffin as well as selections from *The Book of The Law*. One such extract was the "Gnostic Requiem"—a piece which produced a magisterial complaint from Brighton Council.

The last few months of Crowley's life were his most bitter. He was merely a broken old man with a large number of unpleasant memories. He had practiced what he had preached, and his Satan worship was intense. Crowley created his own hell on earth and it made the lives of his followers—and eventually himself—intolerable. Yet the community at the abbey, dark as it was, had its moments of happy naivete and there is no doubt that Crowley had some warm, personable aspects to his character. The trouble is that having devoted himself to satanism, he took care not to let any chink of human quality shine through his personality—and in this he almost succeeded.

Crowley was no magician, but his power of personality was immense.

This explains the many visions and incredulities he summoned up for his associates or acquaintances. In the latter category, Oliver Marlow Wilkinson recalls a strange episode concerning Crowley's powers of suggestion related to him just after the Second World War:

> I had been speaking at a conference in a Gloucestershire mansion, and had then called on a group of artists in an adjoining house. There, over the fireplace, was a large picture of clergymen being hunted over gravestones by devils: the painter obviously on the side of the devils. "I can almost *see* Aleister Crowley standing against that painting," I said, not knowing if my hosts would recognize the name.

"You *would* have done if you had been here when Crowley was with us," said the scene-designer, the leader of the group. When I, in discussing Crowley, doubted his magical powers, the scene-designer said, "You would not have thought that if you had been with us when Crowley was here. After dinner, we came down to a room on the first floor—" he took me to the room—a small one for such a large house—with french windows opening on to rough grass, and trees beyond. "Crowley sat on his haunches, there by the fire. One of us sat on the floor, the other side. Two others besides myself were in the room. As Crowley talked, the man on the other side of the fireplace from Crowley fell sideways, his head a few inches from the flames, and stayed there. Another got up, dropped on all fours, sniffed round the chairs, begged, barked and whined, scratched at the door and the man over there got up, without a word, rushed through the window, and didn't come back till noon next day, his clothes torn, and his face bleeding. I couldn't move for a while, and when I did, Crowley had gone to bed."

"Crowley might have used drugs," I suggested. "And hypnotism," added the young man who was not, I realized, as credulous as I had thought. That, too must be remembered, that Crowley was skilful in the use of drugs; and in hypnotism. "But he used something else, too," added the young man. "What?" I asked. "Magic," said the young man.

But magic was just what Crowley did not have—unless one counts his extraordinary magnetic personality. Aleister Crowley put everything he had into his all-embracing commandment Do What Thou Wilt. He experienced everything self-indulgence could provide—and he under-

95

went every physical and mental sensation possible. But life did to him as it willed—and washed him up in the obscurity of Hastings, desperately reliant on heroin to ensure his own stability and to re-create those sensations that he still needed so much.

* * *

Charles Manson is a very different satanist from Crowley. After the Tate–La Bianca murders he said:

> Mr. and Mrs. America—you are wrong. I am not the King of the Jews nor am I a hippie cult leader. I am what you have made of me and the mad dog devil killer fiend leper is a reflection of your society. . . . Whatever the outcome of this madness that you call a fair trial or Christian justice, you can know this: In my mind's eye my thoughts light fires in your cities.

Sandy, another member of the Family, is particularly expressive of Manson's possession of her when she says:

> Whatever is necessary, you do it. When somebody needs to be killed, there's no wrong. You do it, and then you move on. And you pick up a child and you move him to the desert. You pick up as many children as you can and you kill whatever gets in your way. That is us.

When the Family entered the Polanski house on their murderous visit, one of their members, Tex, was challenged by one of their victims, Voytek Frykowski, who said: "Who are you and what are you doing here?" Tex replied, "I am the Devil and I'm here to do the Devil's business."

96

Manson, whose background was highly criminally disturbed, was described in a report during his adolescence as follows: "Charles is a 16-year-old boy who has had an unfavorable family, if it can be called family at all." The caseworker came to the conclusion that Manson was "aggressively antisocial."

Charles Manson's demonic "adopted" family knew that he was very keen on quoting from the Bible. Ominously, his most favored quotes came from the ninth chapter of the Book of Revelations. His interpretations were wide, to say the least.

In Manson's view, the four angels were the Beatles, whom Manson thought to be "leaders, spokesmen, prophets." "And he opened the bottomless pit . . . And there came out of the smoke locusts upon the earth; and unto them was given power" also referred to the Beatles as did the phrases "Their faces were as the faces of men" yet "they had hair as the hair of women." "Fire and brimstone" issued from the mouths of the angels and this, Manson considered, was a clear reference to the lyrics, i.e., the power—that came out of their mouths. Electric guitars were "breastplates of fire," dune buggies were "like unto horses prepared unto battle" and the Straight Satan motorcyclists associated with Manson were the "horsemen who numbered two hundred thousand thousand." Everything was relative—any meaning could be sought. For instance, the text "And it was commanded them that they should not hurt the grass of the earth, neither any green thing, neither any tree; but only those men which have not the seal of the forehead" was interpreted by Manson to mean that he would be able to discern a mark somewhere on the bodies of his potential victims and by looking at this mark he would be able to tell who was for him or against him. Another verse spoke of worshiping demons and idols of gold and silver and bronze. Manson claimed this referred to the material worship of money, automobiles and houses. Finally, Verse 15 read: "And the four angels were loosed, which were prepared for an hour, and a day, and a month, and a year, for to slay the third part of men." Paul Watkins, in reply to a question referring to this verse in court, replied "He said that these were the people who would die in Helter Skelter . . . one third of mankind . . . the white race."

In Manson's mind the fifth angel was the dead Beatle Stuart Sutcliffe, who had died in Germany in 1962. But to the Family it was Manson himself who was the fifth angel—the ruler of the bottomless pit. "And the fifth angel sounded, and I saw a star fall from heaven unto the earth; and to him was given the key of the bottomless pit."

Manson was not exactly a direct satanist although some of his earlier influences certainly led him toward religious obsession as prosecuting counsel Vincent Bugliosi pointed out in his opening speech. Bugliosi writes:

> We believe there to be more than one motive. Besides the motives of Manson's passion for violent death and his extreme anti-establishment state of mind, the evidence in this trial will show that there was a further motive for these murders, which is perhaps as bizarre, or perhaps even more bizarre, than the murders themselves.

Bugliosi went on to say that the evidence would show how Charles Manson was fanatically obsessed with Helter Skelter. An avid follower of the Beatles, Manson believed that they were speaking to him across the ocean through the lyrics of their songs. Indeed, Manson told his followers that he had found complete support for his philosophy in the words of some of their songs. Naturally the Beatles had no intention of communicating this kind of philosophy.

Bugliosi stated that to Manson, Helter Skelter signified the black man rising up and destroying the white race. The exceptions to this mass destruction were Manson and his chosen followers, who intended to find sanctuary in the desert, living in the bottomless pit of Revelation 9.

Evidence from several witnesses would show that Charles Manson not only hated black people but also the white establishment, whom he referred to as pigs. The word pig was discovered printed in blood on the outside of the front door of the Tate house. The words "death to pigs", "helter skelter" and "rise" were found printed in blood inside the La Bianca house (the Family's second set of victims).

Bugliosi then pointed out that the evidence would also show that one of Manson's principal motives for the seven savage murders was to ignite Helter Skelter—in other words, to start the black-white revolution by making it look as though the black man had murdered the seven Caucasian victims.

In his twisted mind, he thought this would cause the white community to turn against the black community, ultimately leading to a civil war between blacks and whites, a war which Manson told his followers would see bloodbaths in the streets of every American city, a war which Manson predicted and foresaw the black man as winning.

Bugliosi stated that once they had destroyed the white race, the black people would be unable to maintain power because of inexperience and would therefore have to translate this power to the white people who had escaped the holocaust—Charles Manson and his Family.

One of the earlier influences on Manson was Scientology. He told Bugliosi that he had reached the stage which is known as "beta clear." He was also linked with The

Process, or the Church of the Final Judgement. Robert Moore, a former disciple of Scientology, was the leader of the group, and his cult name was Robert De Grimston. Brother Ely (or Victor Wild as he really was) was one of Moore's most ardent followers. Up until December 1967 Wild's house and the San Francisco headquarters of The Process was at 407 Cole Street, in the renowned hippie quarter of Haight-Ashbury. From approximately April till July 1967 Manson and the beginnings of his Family lived some two blocks away. Bugliosi claims that Manson knew Moore and that Manson said to Bugliosi, "You're looking at him. Moore and I are one and the same."

Later Bugliosi met two members of The Process movement who assured him that Manson and Moore had never met and that Moore was strictly opposed to violence of any kind. Later both members appeared on Manson's prison visiting list—although their discussion remained unknown, for Manson became evasive when questioned by Bugliosi.

There are various parallels between Manson's preaching and that of The Process. Both believed that the world would end with an Armageddon in which all but the chosen few would die. Both used the Book of Revelations as a basis for this. Both argued that the Hells Angels motorcycle gangs would be the storm troops of those last days. To The Process, there were three main Gods—Jehovah, Lucifer and Satan, with Christ as the final unifier. Manson had a simpler duality—to his followers he was both Christ and Satan. Both sects preached the Second Coming of Christ, although The Process pamphlet had this to say of it: "Through Love, Christ and Satan have destroyed their enmity and come together for the End: Christ to Judge, Satan to execute the Judgement." Manson, however, preached that the Romans (the establishment) were those who would be crucified.

Other similarities between Manson and The Process were Manson's description of a bottomless pit in comparison to The Process's description of a bottomless void. Within the organization the Process referred to its members (until 1969) as the Family, and the symbol of The Process is slightly similar to the swastika that Manson carved on his own forehead. Among other similar concepts were such statements as "The time of the End is now . . . The Ultimate Sin is to kill an animal . . . Christ said love your enemy. Christ's enemy was Satan. Love Christ and Satan . . . The Lamb and the Goat must come together. Pure Love descended from the Pinnacle of Heaven, united with Pure Hatred raised from the depths of Hell."

Bugliosi states: "These are only some of the parallels I found. They are enough to convince me, at least, that even if Manson himself may never have been a member of The Process, he borrowed heavily from the satanic cult." But Bugliosi is too sweeping here, for there is no evidence to indicate that The Process was in any way a "satanic cult."

But it was not just The Process that possibly influenced Charles Manson. There were influences from at least two other members of the cult—and both of these influences were demonic. Dr. Joel Hockman writes in a psychiatric report on Family member Susan Atkins, on a period of her life in San Francisco apparently somewhere around 1967 or 1968—before she had met Manson. A part of the report reads:

At this time she entered into what she now calls her Satanic period. She became involved with Anton La Vey,* the Satanist. She took a part in the commer-

---

* See later in this section.

cial production of a witches sabbath, and recalls the opening night when she took LSD. She was supposed to lie down in a coffin during the act, and lay down in it while hallucinating. She stated that she didn't want to come out, and consequently the curtain was 15 minutes late. She stated that she felt alive and everything else in the ugly world was dead. Subsequently, she stayed on her "Satanic trip" [for] approximately eight months. . . .

Another Family member, Bobby Beausoleil, was involved with filmmaker Kenneth Anger, who was also involved with the occult and the mystique of the motorcycle gangs. Before he met Charles Manson, Beausoleil starred as Lucifer in Anger's film *Lucifer Rising*.

There were, of course, many other influences on Manson, including Hitler, and Bugliosi writes: "I do believe that if Manson had the opportunity, he would have become another Hitler. I can't conceive of his stopping short of murdering huge masses of people."

The Antichrist has been much prophesied, and in the New Testament Matthew says: "For there shall arise false Christs, and false prophets, and shall show great sights and wonders; insomuch that, if it were possible, they shall deceive the very elect. . . . Wherefore, if they shall say unto you, Behold, he is in the desert, go not forth. . . . "

Charles Manson said, "I may have implied on several occasions to several different people that I may have been Jesus Christ, but I haven't decided yet what I am or who I am." Whatever he was, Manson was neither Christ nor the Antichrist, yet some people have believed him to be both. Manson was a man who sought ultimate power—and achieved it by his complete domination of his Family. Charles Manson was unique—he made people kill for him.

* * *

Fortunately, Manson's influence has not extended outside his own Family. Crowley's, however, did. He was a considerable influence on both Gerald Gardner and Alex Sanders—two practicing satanists who spearheaded the world of British witchcraft. Crowley's sexual magic was of particular importance to Gardner and it is possible that he created "Wicca"—witchcraft in a religious form—to satisfy his own sexual desires. Nudity and flagellation were predictably on the list of rituals and these were somewhat coyly referred to in his writings. The "fivefold kiss" was referred to by the capital letter S, while the same letter with an oblique stroke running through it signified flagellation.

Gardner went unloved by his parents, being put in the care of an Irish nanny with a penchant for travel. At the early age of seven, he accompanied her to the Canary Islands, North Africa, Ceylon and Colombo, where she settled down and married. Gardner grew up in the East, and he lived mainly in Ceylon, Borneo and Malaya, where he became interested in mysticism and the occult, mainly inspired by native practice and custom.

Like Crowley, Gardner gave himself a number of false qualifications and, in the steps of the master, he was a tremendous snob, tracing his ancestry somewhat shakily back to Simon Le Gardenor of 1379. A lifelong member of the Folk-lore Society, Gardner was also an aspiring academic, although many of his papers were of the "scissors and paste" variety. He published a novel and two derivative books on witchcraft—*Witchcraft Today* (1954) and

The Meaning of Witchcraft (1959). He lived in England
after his retirement and joined a witch coven in Christ-
church, Hampshire. Like Crowley, Gardner had considerable persona, and Stewart Sanderson, director of the Institute of Dialect and Folk Life Studies at Leeds University,
remembers meeting him in the 1950s at an International
Congress on Maritime Folklore and Ethnology, held in
Naples. Sanderson remembers:

> He appeared with his wife; he wore an extraordi-
> nary snake bangle on one wrist and one day I actually
> saw a fisherman make the *cornuta* sign against the
> Evil Eye as Gardner crossed over from the tram stop.

Gardner died while cruising around the North African
Coast. He was eighty.

Alex Sanders actually met and was taught by Crowley.
Originally initiated into witchcraft by his grandmother,
Sanders has been elected King of the Witches in England
by members of over 100 covens. At ten, his grandmother
took him to London and left him with a man she called
"Mr. Alexander," who lived in a small boarding house.
"Mr. Alexander," whom Sanders later knew to be none
other than Aleister Crowley, told the child he was a master magician and proceeded to involve him in a ritual
which he termed the Rites of Horus. Crowley then gave
to Sanders' grandmother a ring which was to be held in
trust for him. The ring was originally owned by the nineteenth-century French magician Eliphas Levi.

Once again, Alex Sanders' personality is highly magnetic, although he is aware of its dangers. His grandmother apparently used her witchcraft for good, and Sanders is
conscious of letting her down. He relates:

I made a dreadful mistake in using black magic in an attempt to bring myself money and sexual success. . . . I was walking through Manchester and I was accosted by a middle-aged couple who told me I was the exact double of their only son, who had died some years previously. They took me into their home, fed and clothed me, and treated me as one of the family. They were extremely wealthy and in 1952, when I asked them for a house of my own, with an allowance to run it on, they were quite happy to grant my wishes. I held parties, I bought expensive clothes, I was sexually promiscuous; but it was only after a time that I realised I had a fearful debt to pay. . . . I felt ashamed of betraying my grandmother's teaching. It took me a long time to purge my guilt and purify myself, through the medium of magical ceremonies.

However crazy the magical theories of Crowley and Gardner, there is no doubt that their greatest satanic power was their personality. In both cases it was so strong that both victims and followers were drawn into the net.

In the United States, however, satanic work is much more direct. Anton Sandor La Vey is founding member of the Church of Satan. Born in Chicago in the thirties, La Vey worked as a boy in the funfair and carnival business, as well as being a lion tamer, palm reader and calliope player for the Clyde Beatty circus, giving him the good sense of showmanship so essential to running the Church of Satan. His costume is the essence of this—a black Devil's cap with plastic horns, a black velvet suit and a long red cloak. La Vey claims that his satanic religion is devoted to the enjoyment of all earthly pleasures.

This requires a steady income, and La Vey's followers pay $20 for a life membership of the Church of Satan—and there are over 10,000 members.

La Vey's activities first came to the attention of the authorities when he conducted a satanic funeral for one of his followers—a young U.S. Navy man who had died in a car accident. Amazingly, a naval guard of honor stood rigidly to attention as La Vey went through his doubtful rites. Accompanied by seven black-robed acolytes, La Vey's words eventually caused a massive public outcry— and excellent publicity for the Church of Satan:

> By all the powers of Satan and Hell you will walk this earth to which I bind you forever and ever. And may this plot of ground lie all the way to hell.

La Vey gathered around him, in the sixties, a fashionable enough group of followers. There was the film star and sex symbol Jayne Mansfield, the novelist Stephen Schneck and the "underground" moviemaker Kenneth Anger. Anger introduced even more Crowley influence into the group. One of his films, for instance, entitled *The Inauguration of the Pleasure Dome*, was intended to be an interpretation of Crowley's *Thelema*.

By the mid-sixties the Do What Thou Wilt philosophy of Crowley was being expressed in La Vey's pamphlets as "Man must learn to properly indulge himself by whatever means he finds necessary . . . only by doing so can we release harmful frustrations, which if unreleased can build up and cause many real ailments."

Hans Holzer went along to one of La Vey's services— and describes the following dramatic entrance:

> Now one of the other black-robed fellows handed the leader a small cup. Someone played the organ all

during this opening ceremony, but it was not, of course, La Vey himself, who had not yet appeared among his flock. The music was properly atmospheric and reminded one of the old background music for Hiss the Villain in an old-time music hall. The cup, it developed, contained a mixture of semen and urine, the Satanists' answer to holy water. With a dispenser in the shape of a human phallus, the man in the black hood then sprinkled the congregation with this mixture, while a bell rang in short intervals to announce the opening of the service. The stage was set for the entrance of the high priest, Anton Sandor La Vey.

After the appropriate organ music cue, he strode in with showmanly stance, dressed in a tight-fitting black headpiece with red horns and wearing a black robe over black leotards. Taking the sword from the high priestess, he addressed the four corners of the room. "In nomine dei Satanas, Lucifer excelsi! In the name of our great god, Satan Lucifer, the ruler of the Stygian pits, I command thee to come forth out of the black realms. Come forth, in the name of the four dark princes of hell, Satan! Lucifer! Belial! Leviathan! Satan, take the chalice of ecstasy . . . which is filled with the elixir of life . . . and instill it with the power of the Black Magic . . . which diffuses and supports the universe. . . . " With that, the high priest was handed a chalice from which he drank a toast to the Prince of Darkness. He then placed the chalice right on top of the pubic area of the girl on the altar, where it rested comfortably for the rest of the service.

To La Vey's Church of Satan, the seven deadly sins were regarded as life-giving virtues, and chastity was regarded as unnatural and "evil." Jayne Mansfield went on record as saying that chastity was "a sickening perversion, really evil." She also added that the notion of incubi and succubi had been created by the "filthy imaginings of Catholic monks who had forced themselves to avoid copulation." Gradually she became more and more impressed by La Vey. Meanwhile her lover—and lawyer— Sam Brody, did his best to break the association, claiming that it was bad for Jayne's public image to be associated with the Church of Satan. This seemed reasonable enough, although Brody's motives were probably rather more subjective. Brody tried to blackmail La Vey, but blackmailing satanists is counted as admission of evil deeds or wrongdoing and is very much of a plus factor. La Vey told Brody that he could publish whatever he liked about him or the Church of Satan. At the same time he cursed him—a practice in which La Vey was a self-styled expert. A few weeks later Brody had a minor accident and La Vey was delighted by the coincidence—or the power of suggestion. Later La Vey pointed out that he had received a spirit message—warning Brody and Mansfield of another motor accident—but this time a fatal one. Ignoring the warning, Jayne Mansfield was decapitated two weeks later when Brody crashed the car in which she was a passenger. Brody was also killed.

La Vey was genuinely distressed by Jayne Mansfield's grisly death, but this did not prevent his pushing himself and the Church of Satan to further heights of publicity. Thanks to his show business connections La Vey landed the part of the Devil in Polanski's film *Rosemary's Baby*, and he also created a nightclub act called Anton La Vey and his Topless Witches.

None of this blatant exploitation helped La Vey to win across to the Church of Satan serious recruits for the world of his witchcraft. Most of his followers are vicarious, and it is significant that among the dedications in La Vey's publication *The Satanic Bible*, the name of Phineas Taylor Barnum appears. Most contemporary witches keep a good distance between themselves and the Church of Satan. They realize that La Vey and his wife, Diana, spend much of their time directing satanic weddings, funerals and black masses, surrounded by enough symbolism and artifact to equip a large junk shop. He admits to borrowing much of his magical practice from witchcraft ceremonial. Contemporary witches not only resent this, but firmly state that La Vey's magic is no more than a gimmick—a method of releasing sexual energy and general self-indulgence. Richard Woods, writing in *Soundings in Satanism*, dismisses La Vey's showmanship form of worship. He well summarizes him when he says:

Dr. Anton La Vey seems a bit more reminiscent of John Wellington Wells, Gilbert and Sullivan's sorcerer, than of Cagliostro or Crowley.

It is important to remember that all true satanists regard the Devil not as evil but as the enemy of Christianity. Neither is Satan "good" in this context—at least not in the Christian sense of the word. When worshiping Satan as a God, satanists believe that the God of the Old and New Testament, as well as Jesus Christ, are thoroughly evil—as are their commandments and condemnations. Anything forbidden by Christianity is taken up by the satanist—as so well epitomized by the career of Aleister Crowley. He and his followers, as well as his imitators, hilarious or disastrous as they may have been, were fully fledged satanists to varying degrees. They furthered the existence of hell on earth by actually creating it. They played on the minds of their fellow human-beings and sowed in them the seeds of fear that were to conjure up visions of traditional hell, poltergeist activity, shape-changing and demonry. Anything in the mind is real to the imaginer, and mental dark forces are not to be dismissed as superstition or mental illness. Crowley and his brood *were* able to dominate minds and to fill them with satanic horror. In this sense they were true magicians—and therefore true satanists. "Do What Thou Wilt" is the most succinct charter of the hell that man has created on earth.

PART FOUR

The Black Mass

"With one gesture the man in the black hood yanked the leopard skin off the girl on the altar. She was, of course, nude."

From *The Truth About Witchcraft* by Hans Holzer

I have already discussed the black mass in relation to such celebrators as Crowley, but the actual form of the mass is very traditional—and very dispersed. There are a varied number of rituals under the heading, and the first known and recorded event took place in the seventh century when the Church Council of Toledo condemned an office known as the mass of the dead. The mass of St. Secaire is a classic example and was apparently originated in Gascony. It is essential to perform this ritual in a disused and preferably ruined church, and it is equally essential that the server is a woman with whom the priest has had sexual intercourse.

Continuous prosecutions and the continuous association of the black mass with witchcraft have made the
ceremony notorious throughout the centuries. Satanists
practice it today and despite many local variations and
interpretations, the black mass is basically a blasphemous ceremony that exactly reverses everything in the
Christian high mass. The altar is covered with a black
cloth instead of a white one, the crucifix is hung upside
down, hymns and prayers are sung and recited back-
wards, candles are black, the priest is preferably a defrocked one and whenever the name of God or Christ is
used, it is spat upon or abused. Satan takes the place of
Christ, water replaces wine in the chalice and a turnip or
a similar satirical replacement is used instead of the host.
Sexual rites are a more modern invention, and although
the Devil is seen to be worshiped during the mass, the
origins of the ceremony are more likely to be pagan.

One of the most extraordinary accounts of a black
mass and its repercussions appears in Conway's *Demonology* (1870). It recounts an investigation in 1669 by a
royal commission in the villages of Mohra and Elfdale in
Sweden. The confessions of the so-called witches are
quoted from the Public Register and the result of the
"investigations" was the execution of twenty-three
adults and fifteen children. Thirty-six children between
the ages of nine and sixteen were forced to run the gaunt-
let, and twenty children were lashed on the hands for
three Sundays at the church door.

The "confessions" begin as follows:

> We of the province of Elfdale do confess that we
> used to go to a gravel-pit which lay hard by a cross-
> way, and there we put on a vest over our heads, and
> then danced round, and after this ran to the cross-
> way, and called the Devil thrice, first with a still

voice, the second time somewhat louder, and the third time very loud, with these words—*Antecessor, come and carry us to Blockula.*

Whereupon immediately he used to appear, but in different habits, but for the most part we saw him in a grey coat and red and blue stockings: he had a red beard, a high-crowned hat, with linen of divers colours wrapt about it, and long garters upon his stockings.

The villagers were then asked by Satan if they would serve him with soul and body. When he received acquiescence, he placed them upon a great beast that he had at the ready and carried them over a number of churches and high walls. They eventually came to a green meadow where a satanic place called Blockula lay. There, the villagers had to procure scrapings of altars and filings of church clocks. Then the Devil gave them a horn with a salve in it so that they could anoint themselves. He also gave them a saddle, a hammer, and a wooden nail (to fix the saddle). After these preparations had been made, they were to continue the journey. The confessions continued:

For their journey, they said they made use of all sorts of instruments, of beasts, of men, of spits, and posts, according as they had opportunity: if they do ride upon goats and have many children with them, that all may have room, they stick a spit into the backside of the Goat, and then are anointed with the aforesaid ointment. What the manner of their journey is, God only knows. Thus much was made out, that if the children did at any time name the names of those that had carried them away, they were again carried by force either to Blockula, or to the crossway, and there miserably beaten, insomuch that some of them died of it.

One little girl confessed that as she was being carried away by the Devil she shouted out the name of Jesus. Immediately afterward she fell on the ground with a great hole in her side. Apparently the Devil healed this and continued to abduct her. Even at the time of the confessional, she still complained of a pain in her side.

All the villagers agreed that the sinister Blockula was situated in a large meadow—so large that it was impossible to see its boundaries. There was a house that fronted the meadow with a wildly colored gate. Beyond this gate was a smaller meadow which was used for grazing satanic beasts. Inside the house lay the slumbering masters of the beasts and in one huge room there was a long table where witches sat. In another room there were "lovely and delicate beds."

The first ritual to be observed at Blockula was the black mass followed by a satanic pact. This had to be sworn, and each villager cut a finger and wrote his or her name in the blood in the Devil's book. They were also baptized in the Devil's name and assured that the final day of judgment was at hand. To prepare for this day they were obliged to build a great house of stone. Once inside this, the villagers were told they would be spared the day of reckoning. They would also experience the greatest delights and pleasures inside the house. But there was a major problem—however hard they worked at the house, the walls continually fell down as fast as they built them up.

At this time the villagers saw another Devil much more monstrous than the one that had carried them off. He was in the form of a dragon, surrounded by a great fire and bound with an iron chain. The first and more conventional Devil then arrived and told the villagers that if they returned home and confessed anything at all, the Dragon Devil would be loosed on them, plunging all Sweden into demonic terror.

Some of the Elfdale children talked about a white angel who would appear from time to time, forbidding them to carry out the Devil's instructions. The angel also reassuringly told them that the period of abduction would not last long and was permitted only because of the wickedness of the people. The villagers went on to confess (despite the Devil's threats) that he had entertained them by playing on a harp and would then take various of their number to a chamber where he had sexual intercourse with them. Eventually, the villagers claimed, sons and daughters were produced for the Devil. He then proceeded incestuously to marry these sons and daughters; and their progeny were toads and serpents.

After sexual intercourse a meal was had where those most favored were sat by the Devil's right-hand side, while the children had to stand by the door to be fed with meat and drink by the Devil. After dining, dancing began during the course of which the villagers hurled abuse at each other and began to fight.

The confessions continued with the claim that the Devil had given the villagers a beast about the size and shape of a young cat which was mysteriously known as a "carrier." He also gave them a bird as big as a raven but white in color. These two creatures could be sent anywhere and would return with food or seeds. Whatever the bird returned with could be kept by the villagers themselves, but whatever the "carrier" brought back had to be reserved for the Devil. At Blockula he would distribute the "carrier's" booty as he thought fit. Both the creatures carried the food and seeds in their mouths, and so full did they fill them that they were often obliged to "spue" in several gardens en route back to Blockula. Yellow-gold coleworts grew over the vomit. They were termed the butter of the witches.

The villagers who had had sexual intercourse with the Devil were looked on as witches by the lords commissioners. This latter body then asked the villagers to demonstrate their powers of witchcraft, but they were unable to do so. They claimed that once they had confessed, all their powers of witchcraft disappeared. The Devil had also appeared to them after the confessionals in a predictably vengeful mood. His appearance was particularly awesome, with claws on his hands and feet, horns on his head and a long tail. He conjured up a vision of a burning pit with a desperate hand arising from it, which the Devil mercilessly thrust down again. Then he turned on the villagers, pointing out that this would be their fate if they continued with their confessions.

It is quite clear from this extraordinary fantasy that the villagers could not have concocted such startling images with ease. Either the images were suggested to them by the witch-finders or there was a powerful personality among them who received visions or waking dreams. It is also clear from the confessionals that the villagers were trying to blame their predicament on a demonic take-over, made against their wills, and also were trying to stress their own bravery by confessing despite the Devil's "threats."

It is also quite likely that the entire fantasy sprang out of the only element of truth concerning Blockula—the celebration of the black mass. Possibly some of the villagers had practiced this ritual, and demonic visions emerged from the attendant alcohol, drugs or burning herbs.

A much more recent account of a black mass is given

by Huysmans in his novel *La Bas* (1891). Huysmans claimed to have attended such a ceremony and he certainly describes it with startling realism. The hero, Durtal, is taken to a ruined chapel by a vicarious woman named Hyacinthe. There he finds a conventional altar dominated by an obscene Christ. The neck is stretched upward and there is a sneering smile on the face. He is naked and sexually aroused. The altar boy is seen to smooth the altar cloth with his hands, give his hips a sexual wriggle, draw himself up on one foot as if to fly, and gesture obscenely as he reaches up to light the black candles. Meanwhile the toxic smell of bitumen and resin increase the foulness of the atmosphere. Instead of incense, myrtle, rue, henbane and dried nightshade are burned as well as the strong narcotic thorn apple.

Canon Docre, the old and corrupt officiating priest, wears a dark red chasuble and a scarlet cap, on which are sewn two buffalo horns of red cloth. Underneath this outfit he is entirely naked. As he began the mass, his worshipers inhaled the pungent fumes and began to work themselves up into a frenzy. Durtal notices that the chasuble is of the usual shape but its color is the dark red of blood. In a central triangle a black goat rears its horned head, surrounded by a growth of meadow saffron, pinecones, deadly nightshade and plants with poisonous roots.

Indeed, Huysmans mass has all the most dramatic artifacts of satanism—as do the words of the priest:

> Master of all Slander, Dispenser of Crime's Rewards, Lord of Magnificent Sins and Mighty Vices, Satan, it is you we adore. God of Right Reason, receive the falsity of our tears. You save family honor by abortion in wombs made fruitful in heedless mo-

ments, you tempt to early miscarriages, your midwifery saves the unborn from the agonies of growing up, from the misery of failure.

Support of the poor man strained beyond endurance, tonic of the defeated, you bestow on them gifts of hypocrisy, ingratitude, and pride wherewith to defend themselves against the attacks of those children of God, the Rich.

Lord of the Despised, Satan, Reckoner of Humiliations, Maintainer of Age-Long Hatreds, you alone can stir to action the mind of a man crushed by injustice. You whisper to him well-laid plans for revenge, crimes certain of success, you push him into murders, fill him with the delight of revenge, with intoxication over the sufferings he has brought about, the tears he has caused to flow.

O Satan, Hope of Virility, Anguish of Empty Wombs, you do not vaunt the negativeness of Lenten fasts, you alone receive the entreaties of the flesh, the petitions of families poor and greedy. You lead the mother to sell her daughter, to part with her son. You help loves sterile and forbidden. You bring men to screaming neuroses, you are a leaden weight around the neck of hysteria, the bloodstained inspirer of rape!

Master, your servants beseech you on their knees. They entreat you to secure for them the exquisite joy of crimes undiscovered by the law, to help them with evil deeds of which the secret paths bewilder the mind of man. They entreat you to hear their desire for the agony of all who love and serve them. From the King of the Dispossessed, the Son whom the inflexible Father drove away, they demand glory, wealth and power.

118

The black mass was again made notorious in the late eighteenth century by the Hell-fire Club of High Wycombe, and it continually emerges in the twentieth century. In 1940 the occult writer William Seabrook reported that he had witnessed black masses in London, New York, Paris and Lyons. The form they took involved the reciting of the mass by an apostate priest, with a prostitute wearing a scarlet robe as his acolyte. A virgin normally lay naked on the altar before an inverted crucifix. The chalice was placed between her breasts and the wine sprinkled on her body. After the host was "consecrated" the priest did not lift it high in the air. Instead he defiled it.

Italian black masses were reported in the 1950s, while in the 1960s various black masses were performed in England. One was held in a Sussex church (which had to be resanctified afterward) while another, in Clophill in Bedfordshire, involved necromancy. A skeleton was found inside the church while in the churchyard the graves of six women were found to have been opened.

Richard Cavendish writes in his book *The Powers of Evil:*

> In the Black Mass ritual of one of the present-day Satanist groups, Christ is again denounced as a do-nothing king and coward God, cursed as "the pig" and "that nefarious foul-mouthed Jew" and "that foul imposter" who would deny the pleasures of Almighty Satan's realm and condemn humanity to a life of piety and want, and he is ordered to vanish into the void of his empty heaven.

The satanist conviction is that Christ is a false God and that everything He stands for is evil. Hence the reason for turning the Christian mass obscenely on its head.

119

The dualism of Christianity made it highly convenient for the practitioners of the mass to create Satan as a figurehead and as the ruling lord of the earth. The mass has appealed to a variety of different classes ranging from the idle rich to the disillusioned poor, and from the religious fanatic to the sexually frustrated. The drugs and sex element to the mass only serves to increase a hysteria that is already well founded on the blasphemy of the service. Huysmans describes the near possession that overtakes the worshipers toward the end of the mass:

> . . . the women threw themselves down and rolled on the carpet, one of them, as if moved by springs, threw herself on her stomach and beat the air with her feet, another squinting hideously, first made a clucking noise, then became voiceless, her jaws wide, her tongue sticking to the roof of her mouth. Another, her face swollen, the pupils of her eyes dilated, let her head fall on her shoulders and then, lifting it abruptly, began to tear her throat with her nails. Yet another stretched out on her back, undid her skirt, showing a naked stomach, huge with flatulence, twisted her face into hideous grimaces; from her blood-filled mouth she thrust out her tongue, bitten at the edges, and could not get it back in!

All this is very reminiscent of hysterical possession among primitive tribes or the similar conditions that result from extreme forms of Christian service. The black mass whips its followers into a frenzy of emotion and leaves them limp and both physically and mentally exhausted. To a satanist, the ritual is the ultimate expression of all he believes in, and there is no doubt that it truly echoes Crowley's philosophy of Do What Thou Wilt.

"Our Father, which *wert* in Heaven" is the beginning of one of the satanic prayers of the black mass. But, strangely, God is still indirectly worshiped in the mass, although He is regarded more as a talisman against the unbridled evil of Satan than anything else. Protection was needed against the power of the Devil, and what better to put against it than the power of God.

Nor is the Devil merely worshiped at the black mass— the whole power of demonry is also much sought after. In the Grimoires (the Black Books which are detailed in later chapters) the traditional ritual is clearly laid down— and followed today in the same manner as it was centuries ago. The Grimoire of Honorius, for instance, relies heavily on the Christian mass as a springboard toward the black mass. This Black Book emphatically states that the Christian mass is used purely to protect and empower the officiator.

Primarily the officiator must be an ordained priest (but presumably a defrocked or nonpracticing one) and the ritual must begin with the celebrating of a mass of the Holy Ghost on the first Monday of the month in the middle of the night. This is the mass for Pentecost, commemorating the occasion when the disciples received the gift of speaking in tongues. As a result the officiators of the black mass hoped to gain further inspired power by their own commemoration of the Christian miracle. After the consecration of the host, the satanic priest holds it in his left hand and prays to Christ. Part of the prayer reads: ". . . give to Thine unworthy servant, holding Thy Living Body in his hands, the strength to use that power which is entrusted to him against the rebellious spirits."

121

At sunrise the priest takes a black cock, kills it and rips out its heart, eyes and tongue. These are then dried in the sun and ground down to a powder. The remainder of the corpse is buried in a secret place. At the next sunrise, the priest recites the mass of the angels, which is part of the passion of St. Michael—that great fighter against Satan. This is meant to give the priest protection just in case the demonic powers become too unfettered and unruly.

On the altar, one of the black cock's feathers is placed. The priest takes this, sharpens it, dips it in the consecrated wine and writes with it certain magical characters on virgin parchment. Two days later, at midnight, he lights a candle of yellow wax which is made in the form of a cross, and proceeds to recite Psalm 78, which begins:

> Give ear, O my people, *to* my law:
> Incline your ears to the words of my mouth.
> I will open my mouth in a parable: I will
> Utter dark sayings of old:
> Which we have heard and known, and
> Our fathers have told us.

This is followed by a mass for the dead. At the same time the priest calls on God to free him from the fear of hell and to make the demons obedient to him. Then a candle is extinguished and a young male lamb is sacrificed at sunrise by having its throat cut. The powdered remains of the heart, eyes and tongue of the black cock are ground into the skin of the lamb and the corpse is buried with the following prayer that identifies the slaughtered lamb with Christ:

> Sacrificed lamb, be Thou a pillar of strength against the demons! Slain lamb, give me power over

the Powers of Darkness! Sacrificed Lamb, give me strength to subdue the rebellious spirits! So be it.

More magic signs are then drawn on the virgin paper, more psalms are read and the priest says another mass for the dead. This concludes with the chanting of seventy-two names of great power and, at last, the incantation for the spirits to appear at the black mass.

The blasphemy and the duality made this long, complicated and exhausting process highly charged for the priest, and he, his acolytes and worshipers naturally went through the rituals and sacrifices with disarming excitement.

Devil worshipers also believe that the Devil says his own version of the mass. He leaves out, however, the confession of sins and the Alleluia. The Devil would mumble most of the mass very quickly but would deferentially pause for the collection. The demonic host would then present him with eggs, bread and money. He would then preach a sermon and would after hold up a black host with his own symbol on it rather than that of Christ. He would chant "This is my body" while impaling the host on one of his horns. This was followed by the demons chanting "Acquerra Goity, Acquerra Beyty, Acquerra Goity, Acquerra Beyty." This meant "the Goat above, the Goat below: The Goat above, the Goat below."

After this the worshipers formed a cross or semicircle around the altar and threw themselves on the ground. Each was given a part of the host to swallow and, instead of communion wine, they were given a foul-tasting and deadly-cold medicine. Then sexual intercourse with the Devil took place, followed by a free-for-all orgy.

In reality Devil worship and the black mass have been,

123

and still are, an expression of hatred against Christianity, despite the ambiguity of often seeking its protection. Consecrated hosts are burned, the consecrated wine poured on the floor and the crucifixion mocked. Even more emotively, parts of the mass are read backward and the Lord's prayer altered so as to read:

> Our Father, which wert in Heaven . . . Thy will be done, in heaven as in earth . . . Lead us into temptation and deliver us not from evil.

One case, collected in 1942 by the Spanish writer Julio Caro Baroja, concerned a black mass in the Spanish Basque country. Six men and three women met at a farm, had an enormous feast and then stripped. They boiled a cat in a caldron of soup, drank the soup while reciting incantations, made an altar of planks and then celebrated the black mass, using slices of sausage as the host. In similar situations a particular concoction was substituted for the bread and wine. A standard recipe is excreta and menstrual blood or semen.

The Church brought the Devil to vivacious life when they sought to provide an adversary for God—a figure of such horror that sin and sinners could be kept well in their place of fear. So the Church authorities can hardly complain when Satan is worshiped in the black mass. If only they had avoided personalizing the Devil then there would have been no one to worship. It is so much easier to pray to a man—even if he is the Devil—than to the real dark force that exists in the mind, which is the true evil.

PART FIVE

Satanic Science
and Symbolism

To make three girls or three gentlemen appear in your room, after supper: It is necessary to be three days chaste, and you will be elevated.

The Girmorium Venum   —The True Grimoire

Making a pact with the Devil is the first function of satanic science. The pact normally involves the exchange of the soul for a devilish favor—be it money, a change of circumstances, attacks against fellow human beings, help with the crops or the performing of some dark miracle. Other motives include the acquiring of honor and glory, invisibility, the gift of tongues, and transportation from one place to the other in the twinkling of an eye.

The simplest ritual given in any Grimoire (sorcerer's handbook) is as follows:

The Conjuration of Lucifuge Rofocale

125

At the exact moment of the sun being on the horizon, take an unused knife and cut a wand from a wild hazel tree that has so far not borne any fruit. Two candles are required as well as a bloodstone and two documents. The first is a paper containing a conjuration to the spirit. The second is a demand to the spirit, specifying the exact nature of the help required. Pentagrams are required for protection, a container for incense, writing materials and a brazier containing willow wood which has to burn throughout the rite. There is no need for the construction of a magic circle but a triangle must be drawn on the ground in some remote and inaccessible spot, such as a ruined church or castle. A candle is placed either side of the triangle and at the foot of the triangle a protective name is written such as the name of Christ.

Standing inside the circle, the officiator then begins the conjuration of the spirit:

O Emperor Lucifer, Chief of all the spirits which rebelled, I beg thee to favor me in this conjuration, which I am about to perform to Lucifuge Rofocale, thy Minister. O Prince Beelzebuth, I adjure thee to protect me in this work. O Earl Astaroth, favour me, and permit me tonight to obtain the appearance of the Great Lucifuge, in human shape, and without any evil affluvium. And that he may allow me, in return for the pact which I will sign, the wealth which I am in need of.

O Great Lucifuge, I beg thee to leave thy home, wherever it may be, and come to this place to speak with me. If thou doest not this, I will constrain thee to appear, by the force of the Great Living God, his Son and His Spirit. Do my bidding at once, or thou shalt be tormented for ever by the force of the words of Power of the Great Clavicle of Solomon, which he used to compel revolted spirits to obey him and accept his contract.

Appear, then, immediately, or I shall torture thee with the force of these Words of Power from the Key of Solomon!

AGLON—TETRAGRAM—VAYCHEON STIMU-LAMATON EZPHARES RETRAGRAMMATION OLYARAM IRION ESYTION EXISTION ERYONA ONERY ORASYM MOZM MESSIAS SOTER EMANUEL SABAOTH ADONAY, TE ADORA—ET TE INVOCO. Amen.

Then Satan should appear, saying:

I AM HERE! WHAT DOES THOU SEEK? WHY DOES THOU INTERFERE WITH MY REST? GIVE ME ANSWER.

The officiator then says:

I desire to make a pact with thee, for the purpose of obtaining riches at once. If thou wilt not agree to this, I shall blast thee with the Words of Power of the Key.

But Satan will probably reply:

I WILL AGREE ONLY IF THOU WILT AGREE TO GIVE THY BODY AND SOUL TO ME AFTER TWENTY YEARS, TO USE AS I PLEASE.

Then the officiator hands across the pact with the words:

I promise the Great Lucifuge to reward him after twenty years for treasures given to me. And I sign. . . .

If Satan refuses to cooperate and disappears, the Great Conjuration is to be used as follows:

I conjure thee, Lucifuge, by the power of Adonay the great, to appear at once: and I conjure thee by Ariel, Jehovam, Aqua, Tagla, Mathon, Aorios, Almoazin, Arios, Membroth, Varios, Majods, Sulphae, Gabots, Salamandrae, Tabots, Gingua, Janna, Etitnamus, Zariatnatmis. AEAIATMOAAMVPMSCSICGAJFS.

Satan shall then reappear, saying:

WHY DOST THOU THUS TORTURE ME? LET ME REST AND I WILL GIVE THEE IN EXCHANGE THAT TREASURE WHICH IS MOST NEAR. THE CONDITION IS THAT THOU DOST RESERVE FOR ME ONE PIECE OF MONEY ON THE FIRST DAY OF EACH MONTH. ALSO THOU MUST NOT INVOKE ME MORE THAN ONCE IN EACH WEEK AND THAT BETWEEN THE TENTH HOUR OF THE NIGHT AND THE SECOND HOUR OF THE MORNING. TAKE THY PACT, FOR I HAVE SIGNED IT. IF THOU SHOULDST FAIL IN THE UNDERTAKING, THOU SHALT BE MINE ENTIRELY IN TWENTY YEARS.

Now negotiations can begin.

Finally, the officiator discharges the spirit with the following words:

Dante's Inferno as imagined by Giovanni Pisano e Scuolari. The sculpture can be seen on the Cathedral La Schiera Dei at Orvieto.

The alarming prospect of the frozen depths of Hell. From an engraving by Doré which illustrates Dante's Inferno.

Plunging into the depths. An etching by Schiovonetti based on William Blake's "The Day of Judgment" (British School, 1757–1827).

Satan commands his unholy flock. From an illustration by Pinelli, 1826.

The tortured visions of St. Anthony. From "The Temptation of Saint Anthony" by Martin Schongauer.

Satan in his many forms: as a fallen angel. From an engraving by J. Gavchard.

As a flying fiend. From an engraving by Delacroix.

Satanist Crowley. A photograph taken in 1947.

The mark of the Beast. A typical female disciple branded with Crowley's magical insignia, 1947.

Do What Thou Wilt. A sinister self-portrait of Crowley and his deadly proclamation, 1947.

Medmenham Abbey in Buckinghamshire. The self-indulgent haunt of
Dashwood's Hellfire Club. Engraved by J. Smith from a drawing by T.
Nash for *The Beauties of England and Wales*, published in 1802.

Satan guides his witch crones towards another victim. An anonymous
print published by George Virtue in London in 1839.

The practice of witchcraft as advocated by their satanic master. From the title page of a German book on witchcraft published in Leipzig in 1668.

Cistercian monks assisting in the expulsion of devils by flagellation. From a painting by W.F. Yeames in 1867.

Exorcism in the Castle of Cappelin in Austria in 1574. The anonymous engraving shows a woman being freed of the evil spirits that were possessing her.

The traditional spirit of Satan is released from its victim by Saint Remy.

Go in peace, and peace be with you. Come whenever I shall call. Amen.

This ritual was laid down in the most notorious of all the Grimoires—The True Grimoire—and can be said to be the standard text. This True Grimoire is an exact key to satanic science and symbolism and the oldest version of it appeared in 1517 published by "Alibeck the Egyption, at Memphis."

However, this would appear to be a pseudonym and the book was more likely to have been published in Rome with an "Egyptian" byline to evade the anger of the authorities. The title page continues with the following wording: "Grimorium Verum . . . translated from the Hebrew (into French) by Plaingiere, Jesuite Dominicaine, with a collection of Curious Secrets. The True Clavicles of Solomon."

It was at this particular time that the Church and the "magicians" were coming to a compromise. Originally clerical opinion had been that all magic outside religious ritual belonged to the black art. Now, magic was being divided into black and white magic—thanks largely to the magical research schools of Arabian Spain. Three main forms of white magic were catalogued. Firstly, the rites and formulae were altered to confirm with Christianity. Secondly, the older form, based anyway on Judaism, was allowed to carry on its way. Thirdly, there was natural magic, which had no link with God and therefore could not be termed sacrilegious. This included alchemy, divining and crystal gazing.

The black art was divided into two condemned areas. The first, which carried severe penalties, was the traditional Christian concept of the Devil, and the pact itself. The second, which did not carry such harsh penalties, involved consorting with demonry in general. The reason for this was that man was considered to be surrounded by demons anyway, and as they were considerably less powerful than Satan, then their allegiance could be bound by the invocation of holy words. The True Grimoire claimed to contain formulae for summoning up these demons. It firmly states that the superior demons are Lucifer, Beelzebuth and Astaroth. In that order their domains are Europe and Asia, Africa and America. Lucifer appears in the form of a fair boy, turning red when angry. Beelzebuth appears in hideous forms ranging from a giant cow to a he-goat with a long tail. When angry he vomits fire. Astaroth appears more modestly as a black human shape. Under Lucifer come two demons: Satanackia and Agalierap. Beelzebuth also has two—Tarchimache and Fleruty. Astaroth has Sagatana and Nesbiros.

Demonry in general runs to many thousands but here is a listing of the most interesting:

Clauneck has power over riches, can cause treasures to be found. Can give great riches to whoever makes a pact with him—is much loved by Lucifer.

Musisin has power over great lords.

Bechaud has power over storms and tempests, rain and hail, and other natural forces.

Frimost has power over women and girls, and will help to obtain their use.

Klepoth makes you see all sorts of dreams and visions.

Khil makes great earthquakes.

Mersilde has power to transport anyone in an instant anywhere.

Clisthert allows you to choose day or night.

Sirchade makes you see all sorts of natural and supernatural animals.

Hicpacth will bring you a person in an instant, though he be far away.

Humots can bring you any book you may desire.

Segal will cause all sorts of prodigies to appear.

Frucissiere revives the dead.

Guland caused all illnesses.

Surgat opens every kind of lock.

Morail can make anything invisible.

Fruitimiere prepares all kinds of feasts for you.

Huictiigaras causes sleep in the case of some, and insomnia in others.

Sergutthy has power over maidens and wives.

Heramael teaches the art of healing, using plants.

Trimasael teaches chemistry and sleight-of-hand. He also teaches the secret of turning base metals into gold and silver.

Sustugriel teaches the art of magic.

Agalierept and **Tarihimal** are the rulers of **Elelogap**, who governs water.

Nebirots rules **Hael** and **Sergulath**. **Hael** enables anyone to speak in any language. **Sergulath** gives every means of speculation.

Proculo can cause a person to sleep for forty-eight hours.

Haristum can cause anyone to pass through fire without being burned.

Brulefer causes a person to be beloved of women.

Pentagnony can cause invisibility, and the love of great lords.

Aglasis can carry anyone or anything anywhere in the world.

Sidragosam causes any girl to dance in the nude.

Minoson is able to make anyone win at any game.

Bucon can cause hate and spiteful jealousy between members of the sexes.

The method of conjuring up the demons, according to The True Grimoire, has to be made on virgin parchment with the character of the demon on it. The intermediary

Scyrlin then arrive and eventually the chosen demon. The summoning involves the following:

1. The Preparation and Purifications of the Officiator:

"Lord God Adonay, who has made man in Thine own image and resemblance out of nothing! I, poor sinner that I am, beg Thee to deign to bless and sanctify this water, so that it may be healthy for my body and my soul, and that all foolishness should depart from it.

"Lord God, all-powerful and ineffable, and who led Thy people out of the Land of Egypt, and has enabled them to cross the Red Sea with dry feet! Accord me this, that I may be purified by this water of all my sins, so that I may appear innocent before Thee! Amen."

2. A knife must be collected and it must be of new steel, made on the day and hour of Jupiter when the moon is a crescent.

Then the Conjuration is recited.

3. Conjuration of the Instrument.

"I conjure thee, of form of the Instrument, by the authority of our Father God Almighty, by the virtues of Heaven and by the Stars, by the virtue of the Angels, and the virtue of the Elements, by the virtues of stones and herbs, and of snow-storms, winds and thunder: that thou now obtain all the necessary powers into thyself for the perfectioning of the achievement of those things in which we are at present concerned! And this without deception, untruth, or anything of that nature whatsoever, by God the Creator of the Sun of Angels! Amen."

Then the Seven Psalms are recited, and afterward the following words:

"DALMALEY LAMECK CADAT PANCIA VELOUS MERROÉ LAMIDECK CALDURECH ANERETON MITRATION: Most Pure Angels, be the guardians of these instruments, they are needed for many things."

The ritual then continues (often with a blood sacrifice) until the demon appears.

There are various other demonic forms of satanic science in the Grimoire, and here are a selection of recipes:

1. *Divination by the Egg:*
   This foretells the future for anyone present during the experiment.
   Take an egg of a black hen, laid in daytime, break and remove germ. Place the egg-germ in clear water in a large glass. Place the glass in midday sun, and recite prayers of the day. With the finger agitate the water so that the germ will move. Allow to rest and then look through the glass to see the answer.
2. *To make oneself Invisible:*
   Take seven black beans. Start on a Wednesday, before sunrise. Take head of a dead man, and put one bean in his mouth, two in his eyes and two in his ears. Bury the head face upward and for nine days before sunrise water with brandy.
   On the eighth day the spirit will appear and will take the bottle and water the head. On the ninth day you will find that the beans are germinating. Take them, put them in your mouth and look at yourself

133

in a mirror. If you can see nothing, the rite has worked.

3. *To see the Spirits of the Air:*

Take the brain of a cock, powder from the grave of a dead man, walnut oil and virgin wax. Mix together, wrap in virgin parchment, on which is written: GOMERT, KAILOETH. Burn it all, and you will see prodigious things. This experiment should be done only by those who fear nothing.

4. *To make three Girls or three Gentlemen appear in your Room, after Supper:*

First be three days chaste, and you will be elevated.

On the fourth day, as soon as you have dressed, clean and prepare your room. You must fast, and make sure that your room will not be disturbed for the whole day. There must be nothing hanging, no clothes, curtains, hats or cages for birds.

After supper, go secretly to your room. Upon the table set a white cloth, three chairs at the table. In front of each place set a wheaten roll and a glass of clear, fresh water. Now place a chair at the side of the bed, and retire, saying these words:

"Besticitum consolatio veni ad me vertat Creon, Creon, Creon, cantor laudem omnipotentis et non commentur. Stat superior carta bient laudem omviestra principiem da montem et inimicos meos o prostanti vobis et mihi dantes que passium fieri sincisibus."

The three people will arrive, and sit by the fire, eating and drinking. If you are a gentleman three girls will come, but if you are a lady, three young men will be invoked. One will sit on the chair by your bed until midnight, and you may ask her questions and she will give you a definite reply on any

134

subject. When she leaves she will give you a ring, which will make you fortunate in gambling.

5. *To make a Girl Dance in the Nude*:

On Virgin Parchment write the Character of FRU-TIMIERE with bat's blood. Put it on a blessed stone, over which a Mass has been said. Then place the character under the sill or threshold of a door which she must pass. When she comes past, she will come in. She will undress and dance, completely naked, until death, if one does not remove the character.

6. *To Nail an Enemy*:

Remove nails from an old coffin, saying:

"Nails I take you, so that you may serve to turn aside and cause evil to all persons whom I will. In the Name of the Father, and of the Son, and of the Holy Spirit, Amen."

Look for a footprint of your enemy, and fix the nail in the middle. Hit the nail with a stone and cover the place with a little dust.

7. *To See in a Vision anything from the Past or Future*:

Write the names in a circle on virgin parchment, before sleeping, and put it under your right ear on retiring, saying the following:

"O Glorious Name of Great God the ever-living, to whom all things are present, I am Thy servant N. . . . Father Eternal, I beg You to send me Thy Holy Angels, who are written in the Circle, and that they shall show me what I want to know, by Jesus Christ our Lord. So be it."

Lie down on your right side, and you will see in a dream what you desire to know.

8. *To Make a Girl come to You, however Modest she may Be*:

Watch for the crescent or waning moon, and make

135

sure you also see a star, between the hours of eleven and midnight. Take a virgin parchment and write on it the name of the girl. On the other side of the parchment, write MELCHIAEL, BARESCHAS. Place the parchment on the earth with the person's name next to the ground. Put your right foot upon the parchment, and your left knee, bent, upon the ground. Then look for the highest star in the sky, and holding a taper of white wax, recite the conjuration, three times. Then burn the parchment, put it in your left shoe and let it remain there until the person comes to seek you out.

9. *To be revenged upon one that has done you hurt*:

Alone after dark, say RAIZINO seven times to the points of the compass. With a blue wood pen write upon a dried, triangular leaf:

R A I Z I
I Z I A R
A Z B G D
B M M T M

Then the leaf must be burned in a flame of a lamp which has not been out for more than three hours at a time. Do this secretly and always carry a quantity of black cord, tied round your right arm.

10. *The killing of men by magic*:

A square with the number seven times seven was made in iron on a plate of lead, and this was hanged in a running river for forty-nine days. Place the talisman in a wooden box together with a widow's tear, the three first stones from the river bank and shoes which had not been used for a year. Then the box was buried. When the spell was needed, the worker made a picture of the things and burned it in a fire of white wood saying EOO EOO EOO MMOO ADAD-

BASANA seven times seven times, and then the man died.

Another method was to write:

MMBAB
BABMM
MMBBA
ABBMM

in white ink on a black cloth, and the man who was to be killed was to wear it near to his body. Then the worker writes it again 25 times on green silk with a black ink. If the man did not wear it he would sicken and die in seventy days. Otherwise he died in three days.

11. *To cause discord between two people*:

Write the square with an iron point on lead:

HDHDH
IDIDI
DHDHD
DIDID

Then sew the square into a leather cover and hang round your neck. Say the words ROUDMO and PHARRUO seven times to each quarter of the globe in a loud voice when you want to create discord. If you want two people to fight say their names and then FIGHT FIGHT ROUDMO. Then they will fight. When you want to stop them say OMDOR.

12. *To obtain the Elixir of Life*:

From the desert seek a stone which is blue on one side and red on the other. When you have found one, take it to a place far away and make for it a sheath of copper and gold, and mount it therein, with a bird inscribed on it, and the words LI LI LI NA NA AN.

Place it in water from a running stream and leave it for seven moons. Then, having bathed and fasted, and carrying new clothes, go to the place. With the stone in your hand say the words again and again and place it on your heart. Then make a fire from your old clothes and put on your new garments. It is better if they are green and white. Then take the water that has been with the stone and it is the Water of Life. Half should be placed in a small container, and carried away with you. The other half is to be drunk when the sun comes up. Then you will live for the period for which you have prayed.

All of these involve some form of pact with Satan and there is no doubt that all would have caused heavy punishments if the practitioners were caught. There were, of course, many other satanic manuals. In most cases they differ in detail as to how to summon the Devil or demonry. *The Black Pullet,* for instance, recommends that the practitioner carry a black hen that has never laid an egg to the crossing of two roads. At midnight the hen has to be cut in two and the following words pronounced over the corpse: *"Eloim, Essaim, frugativi et appellavi."* Then the practitioner's face must turn toward the east. He or she must kneel down and recite the great appellation. While doing this it is essential to hold out a cypress staff. Once this ceremony has been completed, Satan should appear forthwith.

King Solomon was considered to be the *eminence grise* concerned with all dealings with the underworld, and all his many conjurations were used by black magicians throughout the centuries. The wording was in Hebrew but written with Roman characters, and Solomon's Seal was a highly potent magical symbol. More magical circles and signs can be found in the more obscure Black

Books attributed to Pope Honorius such as the *Little Albert* or *The Red Dragon*. More drawings can be found in the Faustian *Höllenzwang* (Hell's Coercion) and several versions of this were said to have been printed in Rome during the pontificate of Alexander VI (1492–1503).

In Amsterdam another Grimoire was printed in 1692 entitled *Dr. Faust's Great and Powerful Sea Ghost*. In the introduction Faust recounts his meetings with Beelzebub, who sent him the servant spirit Mephistopheles. In this case the circle was made with sheet metal, and to summon Beelzebub it was essential to declaim, with every stroke of the hammer "Made strong against all evil spirits and devils." The triangle in the center of the circle had to be made of three chains taken from gibbets and nailed down with nails that had gone through the foreheads of convicted criminals. At the conclusion of the invocation a curse had to be said against Satan which read, "Hound of hell, spirit, precipated in the abyss of eternal damnation; see me standing courageously amidst the hordes of devilish furies." Satan had to be cursed three times before he obeyed the officiatior's demands. Then, when Satan had departed, the instructions were smugly to perform the following: When you have taken possession of the money and the jewels, and Lucifer is gone, then thank God with a psalm. With all your possessions, go to another country. Remain pious. Do not forget the poor and the converts.

There is a certain symbolism for the leading demons, largely laid down in *The Red Dragon* and in the Grimoire of Pope Honorius:

1. Lucifer (emperor): A four-horned head
2. Grand Duke Astaroth: Tongue thrusting forward
3. Lucifuge (chief of the cabinet): Similar to an American Indian
4. Satanackia (chief of the armies): Insectlike

5. Agagliarept (general): Two heads

6. Fleurety (lieutenant general): Sharp profile and clumsily drawn horse-hoof

7. Sargatanos (brigadier): Satanic butterfly

8. Nebiros (field marshal): Leaf and a half-insect-like being

The Red Dragon confides in us a method of summoning up the dead for diabolical purposes. In a chapter entitled "The Great Art of Speaking with the Defunct," an exact formula is laid down: The would-be necromancer must be an assistant officiate at a Christmas mass at midnight. When the host is raised, he must bow down and say quietly, "The dead rise and come to me." Then he must leave the church and briskly enter the nearest graveyard. Pausing by one of the graves, he must say, "Infernal powers, you who carry the disturbance into the universe, leave your somber habitation and render yourself to the place beyond the river Styx." Then, after a short period of silence, he should say, "If you hold in your power him whom I call, I conjure you, in the name of the Kings of Kings, to let this person appear at the hour which I will indicate." Taking a handful of earth and scattering it around him, the necromancer then says softly, "May he who is dust wake from his sleep. May he step out of his dust and answer to my demands which I will make in the name of the Father of all men."

The necromancer then kneels and turns toward the east. He must remain in this position until the sun rises. At this point he must take two human bones and place them in the sign of the cross of St. Andrew. Then the two bones must be thrown into the nearest church. Next comes the complicated part: The necromancer must walk toward the north for exactly four thousand and nineteen hundred steps. Having accomplished this mathematical feat, he must lie down on the ground outstretched. His hands must be on his legs and his eyes raised to the heavens in the direction of the fading moon. Now is the time to summon the dead. He recites, *"Ego sum, te peto et videre queo."* Almost at once the revitalized dead will appear. Once having been used, the specter can easily be dismissed with the words "Return to the kingdom of the chosen. I am happy about you being here."

Finally the weary but satisfied necromancer returns to the grave where he began. With his left hand he must trace a cross upon the gravestone. It is essential to complete this final act or disaster could fall upon him. The final dire warning in *The Red Dragon* underlines this: "Do not forget the slightest detail of the ceremonial as it is prescribed. Otherwise, you would risk falling into the snares of hell."

Manly P. Hall, in *Masonic, Cabalistic and Rosicrucian Symbolical Philosophy* (1936), points out that "ceremonial magic is the ancient art of invoking and controlling spirits by scientific application of certain formulae." Certainly it must be remembered that those seeking Satan's aid also use different hierograms from those seeking God's aid. Devil-seeking symbols are always inverted and the triangle is reversed with the peak facing downward. All satanic rights are made left-hand and the five-pointed star known as the pentagram is also different from its divine shape.

The evil eye is one of the major satanic symbols still in use throughout Europe and South America. It also occurs in the East. There are various protective devices against it, one of which is to raise the hands with the fingers covering one another and putting the hands in front of the eyes. There are thousands of recorded episodes in connection with the evil eye, and the following two ably demonstrate the extent of the belief.

In the late nineteenth century in rural Italy a farmer was reputed to have the evil eye. In the presence of her father, he accidently gave a local beauty a nasty look. Almost at once the girl began to act strangely. She became introverted, refused to go outside and suffered a complete personality change. Forty years ago, in India, a Hindu holy man gave a similar look to a Moslem. In similar style to the Italian girl, the Moslem suffered a personality change, fell ill, was unable to eat and became introverted. These, of course, are typical examples of autosuggestion, rather in the same way that a witch doctor can plant a curse and literally frighten his victim to death. The evil eye, in a less dramatic manner, works in a very similar fashion.

I have already discussed plants in an earlier chapter, but it is worth repeating that another symbol of satanic power is often said to be the mandrake. Certainly, for centuries, it has been an object of superstition. In her *Physica,* St. Hildegard describes the black properties of the mandrake in some detail:

> It is hot, something watery, and formed of the moistened earth wherewith Adam was created; hence is it that this herb, being made in man's likeness, ministers much more than other plants to the suggestion of the Devil; according to man's desire good or evil may be aroused at will, as was done aforetime with idols.

The plant divides into two types, one supposedly made in the image of the woman, the other in the image of a man. The drake in "mandrake" derives from "dragon" in Middle English, and so here is another link with satanism. The description is applied to all strong plant roots thought to resemble the human body, and a narcotic substance can be made from them. Demons are believed to live inside the roots and the mandrake is meant to reveal knowledge of the future by shaking its head when questions are put to it.

With all these demonics around mankind, it became more and more important to combat satanic science with talismans to ward off the evil spirits. These are numerous, but the following are said to be the most reliable:

1. *The Magic Circle*: This takes a variety of forms and is a protective girdle against evil spirits. No invocation must ever be made outside the circle, which is either drawn or indicated by a wand. Any spirit entering the circle was at the magician's mercy.

2. *Magic Crowns*: Usually made of wax and wool bound closely together.

3. *Horned Hand*: A sign of recognition among the initiated. The index finger and the little finger were raised while the other fingers were turned down. This shape recalled the heads of devils drawn in the Middle Ages and was used to make the Devil helpless.

PART SIX

Witches and the Devil

Father, Son and Holy Ghost,
Nail the Devil to the post,
Thrice I strike with holy crook,
One for God, one for Wod, and one for Lok

Old Lancashire witches' cure for the ague

Many witches (those dabbling in black rather than white magic) saw their first duty as making a pact with Satan. The following pact is typical and comes from late-seventeenth-century Germany. The witch recites:

Emperor Lucifer, master of all the rebellious spirits, I beseech thee be favorable to me in the calling which I make upon thy great DEMON MINISTER. Having desire to make a pact with him, I pray thee also, Prince Beelzebub, to protect me in my undertaking. O Count Ashtoreth! be propitious to me, and cause that this night the great DEMON appear unto me in human form and without any evil smell, and that he grant me, by means of the pact which I shall deliver to him, all the riches of what I have need. O great DEMON, I beseech thee leave thy dwelling, in whatever part of the world it may be, to come and speak with me; if not, I will thereto compel thee by the power of the mighty words of the great Key of Solomon, whereof he made use to force the rebellious spirits to accept his pact. Appear, then, instantly, or I will continually torment thee by the mighty words of the Key: "Aglon Tetagram Vaycheon Stimulamathon Erohares Retragsammathon Clyoran Icion Esition Existien Eryona Onera Erasyn Moyn Meffias Soter Emmanuel Sabaoth Adomai, I call you, Amen."

The Devil will then appear and say:

I cannot grant thy demand but on condition that thou give me thyself at the end of seven years, so that I may do with thee, body and soul, what shall please me.

The witch should then give the pact to the Devil. The pact must be written on virgin parchment in the witch's own hand and be signed with the witch's own blood.

I promise great DEMON to repay him in seven years for all he shall give me.
In witness whereof I have signed . . .

Witches, from time immemorial, could be said to be identified by the Devil's mark. Historically, this was said to be a literal casting of a mark on a witch by Satan. The anonymous author of The Lawes Against Witches and Conjuration (published "By Authority" in 1645) states

that "the Devil leaveth markes upon their bodies, some-
times like a Blew-spot, or a Red-spot like a flea biting."
At about the same time the Scottish lawyer Sir George
Mackenzie wrote:

> The Devil's Mark useth to be a great Article with
> us, but it is not *per se* found relevant, except it be
> confest by them, that they got that Mark with their
> own consent; *quo casu*, it is equivalent to a paction.
> The Mark is given to them, as is alledg'd, by a Nip in
> any part of the body, and it is blew.

In some cases the mark was deliberately caused by
pricking or cutting the skin until blood came. A red or
blue mark was caused and somewhere in the process
there are the early fundamentals of the craft of tattooing.
In other cases the mark was simply a scar, a mole or a de-
formity such as a secondary set of nipples. Naturally, the
mark appeared on numerous parts of the body and all
kinds of claims were made by witches or their accusers as
to how they had received the identification from Satan.
There is usually a sexual connotation. Indeed, the
witches' sexual relations with the Devil were as important as the pact itself. Modern black witches regard the
"great rite" of copulation between their high priest and
high priestess as absolutely essential to the occasion. Pagan symbolism is also important, and for the witches of
both black and white callings life and death are linked in
nature's cycle. They believe in a unity of opposites (dualism yet again), so that to worship one is to worship the
other. Also to achieve orgasm is to celebrate both.

Much of the philosophy of the modern witchcraft
movement (as laid down by Gerald Gardner) is preoccupied with death and rebirth. He does not regard the god
of the witches as Satan, but as "the god of the next world,

or of death and resurrection, or of reincarnation, the comforter, the consoler. After life you go gladly to his realms for rest and refreshment, becoming young and strong, waiting for the time to be reborn again."

This is based on the myth of Persephone. The goddess of the witches, a virgin, goes to the underworld to solve the mystery of death. The guardian of the gates forces her to strip herself of all her clothes and jewels, because she is not allowed to bring anything into the land of the dead. Naked, she is bound and scourged. As a result of this she cries out, "I know the pangs of love." Death replies "Blessed be" and throws his arms around her. He then teaches her all the mysteries of life and death and they fall in love. He also teaches her magic. Then Gardner writes that Death says to the goddess of the witches: "But to be reborn you must die and be ready for a new body; to die you must be born; without love you may not be born, and this is all the magic."

But outside the Gardnerian movement, the Devil was much more directly associated with witchcraft. He occasionally appeared to prospective witches in animal shape, but far more usually he appeared as the Man in Black. Taking the initiative, he would offer a pittance for her soul, seal the bargain in blood and consummate the relationship with sex. But this was rarely a pleasant experience. Sexually Satan was meant to be very cold and he did not appear to have the normal masculine sexual functions. His penis was covered in scales and he spoke in a sepulchural voice.

One of the principal and regular dates in the witches' calendar is the Sabbat, and this is still widely celebrated today. In the past the Sabbat was also a part of the imagination. Sixteenth-century witch-hunter Nicolas Remy said that he was willing to agree that some, at least, of the witches' meetings existed in their dreams only. He quoted a witch named Catherine Prevotte as saying, "Sometimes witches are fully awake and actually present at these assemblies: but that often they are merely visited in their sleep by an empty and vain imagination." But imagined or not, like the black mass, the ceremonies took a basic form. The name Sabbat seems to have association with another persecuted group, the Jews, and in early times the witches' meetings were referred to as the "Synagogue."

During the ceremony the witch had sexual intercourse with the Devil, who usually appeared as a goat or in some other animal form. Failing an actual appearance, Satan was understudied by a man dressed up. He is greeted by the witch with a kiss on the backside. Meetings are normally held outside, although smaller groups have been known to gather in a house or a church. There are few reports of broomstick riding, although once it was established that the witch was truly in league with the Devil, then it became widely acknowledged that travel was no problem and demonic animals, reeds, or wisps of straw could equally well serve the purpose. Flying ointment was also used as a further aid to transport.

After the obscene kiss, the witches then reported their evil deeds. In return, they received guidance. King James's *Demonology* lays down the guidelines for this. "At what time," he says, "their master enquiring of them what they would be at, every one proposes unto him what wicked turn they would have done, either for obtaining of riches, or for revenging them upon any whom they have malice at, who granting their demands (as no doubt willingly, he will, since it is to do evil) he teacheth them the means whereby they may do the same."

The next part of the ceremony involves new recruits being presented to the Devil. They are obliged to renounce Christianity and swear allegiance to him. There then followed any marriages or baptisms. Curious postures are also part of the Sabbat, and Guazzo, in his *Compendium Maleficarum* (1626) reveals that:

> When these members of the devil have met together, they generally light a foul and horrid fire. The devil is president of the Assembly and sits on a throne in some horrid shape, as of a goat or a dog: and they approach him to adore him, but not always in the same manner. For sometimes they bend their knees as suppliants, and sometimes stand with their backs turned up, and sometimes kick their legs high up so that their heads are bent back, and their chins point to the sky . . . they turn their backs and going backwards like crabs, put out their hands behind them to touch him in supplication. When they speak, they turn their faces to the ground: and they do all things in a manner foreign to the use of other men.

Feasting and dancing followed the ritualistic part of the ceremony, and the Man in Black sat at the high table, accompanied by his favorite witch of the moment. Remy states in his *Demonolatry* that "his banquets were so foul either in appearance or smell that they would easily cause nausea in the hungriest and greediest stomach. . . . And for drink he gives them in a dirty little cup wine like clots of black blood." He goes on to say that "the dances which were in ancient days performed in the worship of demons [pagan deities] are still used at their nocturnal assemblies." In general the dancing rose to orgiastic frenzy and, again, sexual intercourse, usually with the Devil, concluded the festivities.

Another demonic festival is still celebrated today—All Hallows' Eve, which was originally a festival of fire, the dead and the powers of darkness. It is celebrated on the evening of October 31, the night before the Christian festival of All Hallows or All Saints Day—a day set aside to commemorate the saints and martyrs. In *The Golden Bough*, Sir James Frazer says that

> throughout Europe, Hallowe'en, the night which marks the transition from autumn to winter, seems to have been of old the time of year when the souls of the departed were supposed to revisit their old homes in order to warm themselves by the fire and to comfort themselves with the good cheer provided for them in the kitchen or the parlour by their affectionate kinsfolk. It was, perhaps, a natural thought that the approach of winter should drive the poor, shivering, hungry ghosts from the bare fields and the leafless woodlands to the shelter of the cottage with its familiar fireside.

Bonfires were a familiar feature of Halloween, and demons and witches (reported to be flying in sieves or eggshells) haunted the night. The "guisers"—those who dressed up in masks and horrifying costumes—danced the night away, determined to keep the evil spirits at bay. The tradition is very much maintained by modern witches. In 1963, for instance, witches celebrated the rite at St. Albans in England. Naked save for a string of beads, the high priestess drew a magic circle on the ground with the point of her knife. A candle was lit in each quarter of the circle, while a fifth candle burned on an altar in the middle of the circle. They were not anti-Christian, however, claimed the group. "We just have other means of spiritual satisfaction. It's hard to explain that satisfaction."

Witchcraft today is allowable, although witch-hunting has never entirely petered out. However, it is not on the same scale of persecution as in the Middle Ages. Then,

150

burnings were prolific as this list from the bishopric of Würzburg illustrates:

The Sixth Burning, six persons:
    The steward of the senate, named Gering
    Old Mrs. Canzler
    The tailor's fat wife
    The woman cook of Mr. Mengerdorf
    A stranger
    A strange woman
The Eighth Burning, seven persons:
    Baunach, a senator, the fattest citizen in Würzburg
    The steward of the dean of the Cathedral
    A stranger
    A knife grinder
    The gauger's wife
    Two strange women
The Eleventh Burning, four persons:
    Schwerdt, a vicar-choral in the Cathedral
    Rensacker's housekeeper
    Stiecher's wife
    Silberhans, a minstrel
The Thirteenth Burning, four persons:
    The old smith of the court
    An old woman
    A little girl, nine or ten years old
    A younger girl, her little sister
The Fourteenth Burning, two persons:
    The mother of the two little girls before-mentioned
    Liebler's daughter
The Twentieth Burning, six persons:
    Goebel's child, the most beautiful girl in Würzburg
    A student who knew many languages, an excellent musician

Two boys from the Minster, each twelve years old
Stepper's little daughter
The woman who kept the bridge gate
The Twenty-fifth Burning, seven persons:
    David Hans, a canon in the New Minster
    Weydenbusch, a senator
    The wife of the innkeeper at the Baumgarten
    An old woman
    The little daughter of Valkenberger was privately
executed and burnt on her bier
    The little son of the town council bailiff
    Wagner, vicar in the Cathedral, was burnt alive
The Twenty-eighth Burning, six persons:
    The wife of Knertz, the butcher
    The infant daughter of Dr. Schultz
    A blind girl
    Schwartz, canon at Hach
    Ehling, a vicar
    Bernhard Mark, vicar in the Cathedral
The Twenty-ninth Burning, five persons:
    Viertel, the baker
    The innkeeper at Klingen
    The bailiff of Mergelsheim
    The wife of the baker at the Ox Tower
    The fat noblewoman

Many witches are not satanic in any way, although Crowley's Do What Thou Wilt could apply to much of their spiritual energy. In America the witch cult is broad-based. It is only in Europe that real demonic overtones still cling.

In America, a coven of Gardnerian witches still practice in Long Island. An ex-chieftain of the group, Ray Buckland, now runs a witchcraft museum, and elsewhere there are photographs of Buckland in full dress—a helmet with antlers and a G-string. In Manhattan, Herman Slater runs a business called The Warlock Shop. Although definitely not Welsh, Slater is an advocate of the Welsh Witch movement and he runs a journal called *Earth Religious News*, which is a kind of forum for witches to swap news and views in. Herman Slater writes of his own sect:

Our high priestess wears a moon crown composed of a copper band surmouted by a silver crescent. When she trains a high priestess who splits off to form her own coven, she becomes a witch queen and wears an all-silver moon crown. Her high priest then becomes the king of the woods, which is the same as the Gardnerian Magus, and receives a copper or bronze crown surmounted by a gold sun disc. Upon initiation we take two names, a public name for outside the circle, and a name for within the circle which is held very secret. My own public name is Hermes. Our name as a high priest cannot be disclosed publicly. Our rituals are very beautiful and very simple. They are a celebration of life and contain no ceremonial magic. We are the children and the friends of the gods, and laugh and love with them. We are not solemn within the circle but freely laugh and enjoy ourselves. Unlike the Gardnerians and others, all of us have an active part in the rituals and the high priest is basically co-equal with the high priestess. At every Sabbath the high priestess draws down the horned god into the high priest. We wear robes and do not use the scourge. The circle is normally cast with a rod. It is opened with appeals to earth, air, and water, and is closed with fire. We possess the original "Great Rite" ritual and when it is used it is used by husband and wife or lovers privately and in sacredness and respect. We do not discriminate against those who within their private lives have found love with those of their own sex. However, we work female to male within the circle. Such sexual discrimination has never been a part of paganism as we see it. There is an inner court coven for the more advanced witches, and an outer court coven for the first-degree witches.

There are dozens of other witch cults and magazines including *The New Broom, The Witches Broomstick, The Green Egg* and *Amerisyche*, the newsletter of the American Society for Astro-Psychical Research. One American satanist who was particularly linked to witches was Dr. Herbert Sloan, who lived in Toledo, Ohio. He was a card and tarot reader as well as being something of a showman. He worshiped the "Lord Sathanas" and had, for thirty-six years, been a witch of the Ophitic Gnostic Set. Hans Holzer attended one of Sloan's ceremonies, held in the Dragon Room, in which Dr. Sloan also lived. The ritual was to celebrate the October full moon. When Holzer arrived the Dragon Room was in semidarkness. Candles flickered, demonic pictures covered the walls and there was also a brass Devil's mask mounted on a brass plate. Eventually Dr. Sloan entered, wearing a black cape and two plastic horns mounted on his forehead. He began the service by ringing a bell and then reciting this incantation, which blended both satanism and witchcraft:

Our Lady of Endor Coven of the Ophitic Gnostic Cult of Satanas is now in Sabbath, and this will be the order of service: the call, which you've just heard, the invocation, the creed, first reading, announcements, supplication, communion, second reading, sermon, benediction and social hour. Let's bow our heads for the invocation. Lord Satanas, we invoke into this covenstead thy sacred presence this Sabbathnight, that thou be with us in understanding,

154

that thou open our ears to hear and understand the things which we should understand, and close our ears and minds to those things which are not pleasing to thee. Thank you, Lord. Nema, Nema, Nema, Nema!*

In England, the demonic tradition in witchcraft is still prevalent: The center of contemporary witchcraft legend and phenomena is the Essex village of Canewdon, although it is now largely the echoes that still reflect the superstition. Situated on a remote part of the Thames marshes, legend has it that as long as the church tower stands, there must be six witches in Canewdon, all under the administration of a master witch. "Three in silk, and three in cotton, one being the parson's wife, one being the butcher's wife and one being the baker's wife." When the last witch dies, the tower is doomed to fall—or vice versa. Satan is meant to continuously harry and pursue the parish priest of Canewdon, although the unfortunate parson is always able to elude Satan as the latter is apt to catch his tail in the hedgerows of the narrow, winding lanes. Also, on neighboring Wallasea Island, a now extinct farm known as the Tile Barn was reputed to be the home of an invisible presence that emanated an ice-cold atmosphere. Legend also related that a black head with horns had been momentarily seen in an upstairs bedroom.

The apparent satanic presence certainly created a welter of superstition and diabolical anecdote in the village. Nowadays, few villagers will go near the crossroads at night, at which traditional point a witch was reputedly buried with a stake driven through her heart. The headless ghost of the witch is said to emerge as a shadowy cloud from the churchyard and to make its way along the

---

*Nema is Amen spelled backward.

road leading to a remote river. Another much accredited legend relates how one of the witches rowed across the local river in a stolen church bell, using feathers as oars. But the bell sank and it is is said that it can still be heard tolling underwater. Near the river's edge there is a barren patch of ground on which nothing will grow. This is said to be the witches' meadow where they came to renew their powers.

The last known record of the six witches was made in the 1880s. The reputed six were:

Mrs. W., a ferociously bad-tempered cripple who cast spells.

Mrs. L., who cast plagues of lice on those who offended her.

Mrs. K., who used to give passersby the evil eye and who tried to prevent anyone entering the church.

Mrs. L., (another one) who refused to step over a doormat under which a silver knife had been laid, therefore exposing herself as a witch.

Mrs. M., who was the mildest of the six and who occasionally materialized by her neighbors' bedsides at night, terrifying them out of their wits and staring at them austerely from underneath a poke bonnet.

Mrs. C., who was renowned for bewitching wagonwheels and possessing imps.

The so-called grandmaster of the unfortunate and no doubt innocent women was an eccentric known as George Pickingill, who was born at Hockley Farm in 1816 and died in 1909. Throughout his life he worked as a farm laborer and for years was reputed to have evil powers. He would openly threaten to bewitch farm machinery at harvest time and would have to be bribed with beer to go away. He was said to be able to summon up the six witches by whistling, and they had to reveal their identities by standing outside their front doors. On the more constructive side, Pickingill was apparently able to harvest a field of corn in half an hour, employing the aid of imps who would do all the work for him while he sat under a hedgerow with his pipe. Poltergeist activity was said to be rampant in Pickingill's cottage and he was able to read minds and to cast spells. As he grew old, Pickingill became a terrifying figure. He was dirty, ragged and incredibly emaciated with eyes that seemed to probe deep into the heart of the soul. On the day of his funeral, as the hearse drew up at the churchyard, the horse apparently trotted mysteriously out of the shafts without any impediment.

Even today there is an old altar tomb in the churchyard where children listen to hear the Devil rattle his chains underneath the earth. The sighting of white rabbits is considered to be great ill-luck as this was purportedly the guise taken (and still taken) by the Canewdon witches. The same applies to the appearance of white mice, which were Pickingill's familiars.

Canewdon boasts another supernatural character, whose descendants are still in the village. Known simply as Granny, she was a defense against black witches. A white witch herself, she created many protective devices for the villagers to use against her satanic counterparts. One particular Canewdon story describes her courage. In the beleaguered church, lighting candles for evening service, Granny noticed a misty figure enter and kneel at the altar in prayer. But Granny had no fear of what appeared to be a faceless woman wrapped up in a gray shroud. Considering that anyone unidentifiable coming into the church must be a holy angel, she knelt beside the figure and prayed. When she opened her eyes the specter had gone.

In the 1970s the Canewdon legends proliferate. Up until the First World War it was considered unlucky to take a wheeled vehicle through the village in case it broke down. Even today children in surrounding villages believe that to cycle through Canewdon will invite a puncture. But it is not just this village that contains so many fears—the whole of the area of Southeast Essex is considered to be witch country.

Witch country lies between the Thames and the River Crouch and has the North Sea as its eastern border. The place is remote, low-lying and marshy. It is only comparatively recently that witchcraft superstition has begun to ebb amongst the largely agricultural population. But even now, amid all this isolation of wind and salt and marsh, many people are still fearful of the unknown. Many of the low flat fields are reputed to be haunted, black dogs prowl the lanes at night and the Devil has many bases from which to maraud and to persecute the local priesthood. Superstition also has it that the Devil is often to be seen wandering mournfully along the sea walls.

Throughout the whole of Essex, there are various landmarks connected with the Devil and witchcraft. There is the Devil's Mouth, an archway at Thorndon Park near Warley, the Devil's Walls at Tolshunt d'Arcy, a house called the Demon's Tenement on Foulness Island, and the tallest thistle in any Essex field is inevitably known as the Devil's Thistle. Numerous sightings of Satan in Essex are typified by this eyewitness account in the south of the county:

He was seven foot high, with one cloven hoof and one ordinary one. His ears were like rhubarb leaves and when they flapped the draught nearly blew me over. He offered me bread and crab-apple and I took it, or he'd have stamped on my feet if I hadn't. I had to have a glass of whisky when I got home, and when I tried to tell my wife about it, she smelled my breath and said that I'd been drinking.

Demonic witchcraft was also involved in the murder of Charles Walton in 1945 in the village of Lower Quinton in Warwickshire. Walton was another agricultural laborer, morose, silent and largely uncommunicative. Rumor had it that the personality change had come across Walton when he was a boy. Always wary of black dogs, Walton had seen a phantom black dog three nights running on nearby Meon Hill. On the third night the dog had changed into a headless woman, and the next day his sister had died. From that moment on Walton had hated dogs. He also began to breed in his back garden big "natterjack" toads. This was a fact—not rumor—for on his death, Walton's back garden was covered with them. His morose and isolated life-style continued until his death. But it was Walton's death that brought the legends of demonic witchcraft back into daily discussion.

He was found, after a day's work, in a field, lying underneath a willow tree. There was a look of utter terror on his face. His own pitchfork was driven through his neck, nearly severing his head. The prongs of the pitchfork had entered his throat on both sides and were embedded six inches into the ground. A cross-shaped wound had also been torn across his throat and chest with another implement—Walton's slash hook, which was then lodged between his ribs.

This barbaric murder brought two investigators onto the scene. The renowned Fabian of the Yard and Dr. Margaret Murray, whose books on witchcraft in Europe had won her an international, authoritative reputation on the subject. Both accepted that Walton's death was a case of witchcraft murder, but tracking down the culprit was to prove impossible. The area was already steeped in demonics, and many local witches, or "wise women," were reported to exist. Also, behind Meon Hill was a curious group of rocks known as the Rollright Stones. Legend claimed that the rocks were really the remains of a Danish king and his knights, all of whom were petrified by a witch who was anxious to prevent them taking over the throne of England. Certainly, the stones were very old and archeologists dated them as belonging to a period some fifteen hundred years before Christ.

Modern witches from Birmingham had held regular meetings around the stones and various ceremonies had taken place. In their investigations, Fabian and Dr. Murray discovered that an ancient defense against a witches' spell was to cut the witch above the nose and mouth, and also to spill the blood, which would neutralize the curse or spell. Then they came across the Haywood case, and this further substantiated the fact that the unfortunate Walton had been the victim of somebody who believed the old man to be a witch. Haywood was a mental defective, living in 1875 in the village of Long Compton, which is very near Lower Quinton. Haywood had become convinced that an old lady named Ann Turner was a witch and had been active against both him and the community in general. He killed Ann Turner by slashing her throat with a bill hook in the form of a cross. Haywood also pointed out, in his confession, that there were an additional sixteen witches in Long Compton, and, if allowed, he would be quite happy to kill them all. It was later discovered by Fabian and Dr. Murray that Ann Turner had also been pinned to the ground by a pitchfork in exactly the same way as Charles Walton.

Dr. Murray then advanced further information, based on her knowledge of centuries of witchcraft practice. She pointed out that Walton was murdered in February, which was one of four months in the year when sacrificial killing had traditionally taken place. Also, the blood from Walton's throat had been allowed to seep into the ground via the prongs of the pitchfork—another example of sacrificial killing. In other words it fitted well into the tradition that if life was taken out of the ground, then it must be replaced by a blood sacrifice. It was also true that the crops had been slow in starting the year of Walton's murder, despite the promise of an early spring. There had been several accidents to local livestock. Also, crop failure and livestock problems had initiated the Haywood killing.

Later a writer named Donald McCormick made another discovery when researching a book on the Walton case, entitled *Murder by Witchcraft*. A reliable source in Lower Quinton told him that Walton indulged in the habit of harnessing some of his pet toads to a miniature plough and sending them across ploughed fields. This was a traditional witches' method of cursing the crops, and the information put the final seal on the certainty that Walton was killed because he was thought to be a witch and in league with the Devil. There was even a historical precedent for the "toad plough." McCormick describes in his book how the Scottish witch Isabel Gowdie confessed to using exactly the same method to destroy or stunt the growth of crops. In 1662 she was burned at the stake for the troubles she brought on local villagers.

Fabian never found the killer of Charles Walton. He lacked the necessary evidence, but McCormick writes that he thinks he knows who Walton's murderer is. In all probability it was someone local—and someone who was aware of the precedent that the Haywood case had set. So therefore in 1945 there was still someone superstitious enough to believe in witches and to further believe that the alien Charles Walton was a practitioner of the black art.

One of the most vivid and disturbing accounts of modern satanic witchcraft is related by a journalist and photographer named Serge Kordiev. Kordiev and his wife had a boat moored in the witch country of Essex. This time the experience took place at Burnham on Crouch near the Royal Corinthian Yacht Club. Shortly before midnight, a few years ago, Kordiev noticed large and expensive cars parked near the sea wall. He also noticed a group of well-dressed people making their way with some stealth down toward the mouth of the River Crouch. Next morning Kordiev traced their footsteps to a derelict farm. There he found the familiar signs of a black magic ritual—the double circle, small triangle, burnt-out black candles, bloodied feathers and the scorched remains of a Bible. Kordiev took some photographs and sent them to a Sunday newspaper, which ran a feature on them. As a result he received some threatening telephone calls and finally an invitation to a black magic ritual. At the same time the caller told him that if the Kordievs joined there would be no "backing out." They were later picked up in a chauffeur-driven car and taken to an outbuilding behind a large Victorian house.

After a few drinks, the Kordievs were asked to strip. They also had to pay an initial subscription of £25 each, plus a £3.3s. initiation fee and £15.10s. for robes and apron. Once inside the ceremonial room they were given black satin aprons to wear, which had as a frontal decoration an orange eye and triangle. The color scheme of the room was in red, black and white. There were black tiles on the floor over which a white pentagram had been superimposed. Heavy red carpeting was hung around three walls while on the fourth a gigantic mural showed a chained and horned monster, surrounded by flames, about to attack a naked girl. Beneath this dramatic illustration was placed an altar with six black candles and, below it, a marble slab. Lighting was provided by a glowing brazier and surrounding it were half a dozen robed and hooded figures. The initiation ceremony began with one of these figures declaiming:

Brothers and sisters, on this occasion two strangers pray for admission to our fold, and it is for you,

162

Disciples of the Prince of Darkness, to say now whether you have or have not any objection or reason why these two persons should not be received into our circle.

This solemn pronouncement was rather anticlimaxed by the tape-recorded bleating of a goat. However, impetus was soon restored by a naked man covered in red oil who stood by the altar. He wore a black Devil mask and was accompanied by two young female acolytes who were wearing black robes. The Kordievs were then told to kneel before the "master" and some form of mild narcotic was thrown onto the brazier, giving off a thick, perfumed smoke. The Kordievs were then asked to promise eternal homage to Satan and to sign the pledge with their own blood. They were then given the satanic names of Frater Capricornius and Soror Gemini. Then the master placed his hand on the Kordiev's genitals and they felt a tingling sensation which could have been caused by a low-power electric current. A back-to-back dance followed, with which the ritual was complete—and the Kordievs returned home. Kordiev remembered:

In the morning the whole thing seemed like a nightmare. But there were dramatic changes in my professional life after that. For a start, the enormous—to me—amount which I had spent in joining the group was immediately covered by unexpected cheques from my agent. I was inundated with requests for work from magazines, and almost everything I touched seemed to turn to gold.

But the satanic pact was to end in tragedy. Having attended a few similar rituals, the Kordievs attended a black mass, of which they strongly disapproved. A young girl member of the circle had been accused of betraying confidences. Because of this she had to form a naked altar while the black mass was said over her. Eventually the master had sexual intercourse with her and a wax dummy which had particles of nail and hair from the "outsider" was placed on the altar. A black cock was sacrificed and members of the circle were obliged to drink its warm blood from a chalice. Later Kordiev discovered that the outsider was a prominent businessman, and that he had died of a heart attack on the same evening as the black mass ritual had been carried out.

Before their "confirmation" ceremony took place the Kordievs decided to leave the circle. But this was not so easy. Their financial luck turned, and Kordiev's wife came near to a breakdown. They moved to remote Romney Marsh in Kent but serious misfortune followed them. A huge toad appeared on the doorstep, maniacal laughter echoed through the house, and much of the interior of the building was mysteriously wrecked. Kordiev said:

> I went downstairs after a restless night to find my retriever cowering in a corner of the kitchen. The studio was a shambles. Drapes and furniture had been torn down and strewn everywhere. The carpet had been stripped back, and the window was broken so thoroughly that the glazing bars had broken under the weight of someone or something bursting out. . . . The place was empty when I locked up. There were obvious signs of a break-out, but no signs at all of how whatever had caused the damage got in. I still think that somehow the incident was caused by an evil power in revenge for our breaking away from the Satanist group.

Worse was to follow: Despite forming a white magic coven, misfortune still occurred in the Kordievs' lives.

164

Then, in 1971, the breakages began again, and there was considerable poltergeist activity. Anne Kordiev appeared to be the center of these disturbances. For a while she seemed possessed and then threw herself from the bedroom window, breaking both legs. Against her will, Serge Kordiev put the house on the market. His wife told him that she would never leave it. Her prophecy was all too correct and a few months later she was dead. Eventually the house was sold to a building contractor who demolished the building owing to its "dreadful atmosphere." Holiday flats were planned in its place but every single time a prospective purchaser was shown around the site, he changed his mind very rapidly. To this day the ominous site remains empty.

Finally, a necessary adjunct to satanic witchcraft is necromancy and the robbing of graves. There are quite a number of contemporary instances of this. For instance, in March 1963 seven tombs in the churchyard of a derelict church on Dead Man's Hill at Clophill in Bedfordshire were damaged. From one of them, the coffin of a girl who had been dead for two hundred years was removed and her bones placed inside the church. On Midsummer night in 1969 another tomb was broken into and attempts were made to dig out the body inside. In the first instance the feathers of a cockerel were scattered among the bones. Grave robbers entered Tottenham Park Cemetery on Halloween night in 1968 and broke open a coffin. The body inside was disturbed, dead and dying flowers were arranged in circular patterns on the central drive and a new grave was uncovered.

In 1974, at the Old Bailey in London, Robert Farrant was charged with unlawfully, maliciously and indecently breaking open and entering catacombs in consecrated ground, interfering with and offering indignity to the remains of a body "to the great scandal and disgrace of religion, decency and morality." Eventually Farrant, de-

165

scribed as an occult high priest, was found guilty of unlawful and malicious damage to a memorial of the dead, and of unlawfully entering a place of interment at Highgate Cemetery, London. He denied all the charges, claiming the damage had been done by satanic cults. During the trial, the jury were told that tombs and vaults were broken open, coffins broken into and corpses taken out of them. The traditional circles and triangles were found chalked on the walls of the vaults. Farrant was alleged to have told witnesses that he required blood and bones for necromancy, and he had sacrificed a cat in Highgate Woods. A witness for the prosecution (described as an "occult specialist") claimed that an attempt had been made to animate the bodies so they could perform some rather doubtful functions, a witness confessed to having pulled a body out of a tomb for a laugh and as a result the police found a headless corpse in the trunk of a car—which started the investigations. The police also claimed that on a visit to Farrant's flat they found an altar draped in black and a drawing of the face of a vampire.

It is not clear whether the demonic art of necromancy was practiced in any of the above cases. The rite itself is dangerous, for practitioners believe that the disturbed corpse could well turn on its tormentor. For nine days before the exposing of the corpse the necromancer and his assistants surround themselves with the aura and artifacts of death. Sex is not allowed, woman are taboo and dress consists of used grave clothes. Diet is equally unpleasant and is composed of dog's flesh (the dog being the symbol of Hecate, goddess of death), unfermented grape juice, and black, unleavened and unsalted bread. Meditation and immobility are also part of the waiting period. On the ninth day the necromancer visits the grave between midnight and one in the morning. There, he begins his preparations. A circle is drawn around the grave and "consecrated." Torches are carried, a second circle is occasionally drawn for protection against evil spirits, and a combination of hemlock, henbane, wood, aloes, saffron, opium and mandrake is burned. The grave is opened, the coffin lid torn off and the unfortunate corpse is exposed. It is then dragged out of its coffin and flung on the side of the grave. Then the necromancer touches the corpse three times and commands it to rise with the following invocation:

> By the virtue of the Holy Resurrection and the agonies of the damned, I conjure and command thee, spirit of——deceased, to answer my demands and obey these sacred ceremonies, on pain of everlasting torment. Berald, Beroald, Balbin, Gab, Gabor, Arise, Arise, I charge and command thee.

After this recitation, the spirit returns to what is left of its old body and answers the necromancer's questions, which are usually to do with divination. Eventually the necromancer rewards the spirit by giving it eternal rest and burns the body. Alternatively he might drive a stake through its heart.

Black witchcraft and satanism are interdivisible. The link is the pact, and the union sexual intercourse. Modern demonic witchcraft is still practiced and the pact is still signed. The only difference is that there is no longer legislation against them and they are no longer persecuted. This is the healthiest sign of all, for in past centuries it was largely the persecutors who sadistically created the witches for various pleasure, as scapegoats and to exploit superstition. Typical of these persecutors and of the mentality of the persecutor is the following description of a sixteenth-century witch-hunter.

> There came then to Inverness one Mr. Paterson, who travelled all over the kingdom trying witches,

and was usually called the Pricker. Stripping them nude, he alleged that the spell spot was discovered and could be seen. . . . He first polled all their heads and collected their hair in the stone dick, and then proceeded to pricking the women with pins. . . . This villain gained a great deal of money and has two servants; at last he was discovered to be a woman in men's clothes. Such cruelty and rigour was sustained by a vile varlets' fraud.

Nevertheless, modern satanic witchcraft, liberated from oppression or not, is still a highly dangerous ritual to dabble in. It is not so much the appearance of Satan that is to be feared, but the demonic acts of those who try to summon him.

PART SEVEN

The Devil Inside You

Smooth devils, horned devils
Sullen devils, playful devils,
Shorn devils, hairy devils,
Foolish devils,
Devils, Devilesses, and young devils?
   From *The Passion of St. Quentin*, a
   fourteenth-century Miracle Play

Throughout this chapter I have discussed the results of exorcisms, credible or doubtful, and the activities of exorcists, credible or doubtful, from the point of view of their belief in possession as an outside force. In fact, I believe possession to be much the same as anything else that is part of the Devil's dominion on earth—i.e., that it emanates from inside the tortured minds of human beings. Although this is not the view of most of the participants in this chapter, it is nevertheless just as demonic in the spiritual sense of the word.

169

Possession and exorcism have been on everybody's lips
since the release of William Peter Blatty's *The Exorcist*.
More importantly, both states have been very much in
people's minds. The film made a profound impression on
most people who saw it. Not because of its horror, not because of its phony science, but entirely because of the
credibility of its composition. The film had a great air of
reality to it in terms of the possession of the girl—and,
later, the awesome results of the exorcism. The established Church made a fool of itself, not for the first time,
by condemning the work, and by its condemnation,
merely increased the audiences.

Dr. Martin Israel is a practicing exorcist. He is also a
Church of England priest. His opinion is that:

> Possession is very much on a sliding scale. Gener-
> ally speaking a person is possessed by a relative or
> friend whose discarded personality is left behind af-
> ter death. The reason for this is that the dead person
> is still demanding something from the living. Gener-
> ally speaking they died feeling angry, or sorry, about
> the living person they eventually possess. All those
> who are possessed are psychic. Also they may have
> previously shown symptoms of mental illness or
> schizophrenia. Sometimes they show depression, of-
> ten influenced by guilt. I have never seen any out-
> ward manifestation of possession except the above
> symptoms. I entirely accept that there can be de-
> monic possession, i.e., possession uninduced by the
> spirit of a dead human being. These cases are rare
> and if I had to exorcise I doubt if I would have the
> strength to perform the ritual on my own—I would

need the assistance of other priests. As to the exorcism itself, I have found in all cases of human possession that I have been able successfully to expel the evil spirit by countering it with love. Only when the spirit is able to lovingly forgive—to come together in spiritual harmony with its victim—then can an exorcism be deemed complete and successful. This can often be achieved in the cases of possession by human spirits—but is very much more difficult with demonic possession. Either way, exorcism is a team effort between the possessed and the exorcist. The power of prayer is our strength and reconciliation our objective.

The Old Testament refers to exorcism only once and that applies to Tobit, Chapters 6–8 and concerns Tobias and Sarah in the Apocrypha. In fact Sarah was guarded by a demon rather than possessed by one, rather like later legends of princesses being guarded by dragons. In the New Testament, disease and possession are often linked as for instance in Luke, Chapter 13, Verse 16, when the woman bent double is said by Christ to be bound by Satan. Christ also gave his twelve apostles the power of exorcism, and Matthew, Chapter 10, Verse 1, reads: "And when he had called upon him his twelve disciples, he gave them power over unclean spirits, to cast them out, and to heal all manner of sickness and all manner of disease." Referring to Christ as exorcist, Matthew, Chapter 4, Verse 24, says: "And his fame went throughout all Syria: and they brought upon him all sick people that were taken with divers diseases and torments, and those which were possessed with devils . . . and he healed them."

Finally, in Acts, Chapter 19, Verses 13–16, exorcists are described:

171

Then certain of the vagabond Jews, exorcists, took upon them to call over them which had evil spirits the name of the Lord Jesus, saying, We adjure you by Jesus whom Paul preacheth.

And there were seven sons of *one* Sceva, a Jew, and chief of the priests, which did so.

And the evil spirit answered and said, Jesus I know, and Paul I know; but who are ye?

And the man in whom the evil spirit was leaped on them, and overcame them, and prevailed against them, so that they fled out of that house naked and wounded.

In Acts, Chapter 16, Paul drove an evil spirit out of a girl who claimed to be able to foretell the future, and once driven out, Matthew, Chapter 12, Verse 43, warns that waterless places are unsatisfactory places for expelled demons as the water was considered their element—and they would become even more malignant when deprived of their natural habitat. Because of this, in very early Christian Church days (about 150 A.D.) there was a blessing and exorcism of the water to be used for baptism.

Unfortunately, abnormal outward manifestation was all too often seen as possession and this has been maintained right up until the twentieth century, still persisting in primitive societies. In other words, the mentally ill, mentally defective and epileptics were all considered to be possessed and were duly exorcised. Pope Cornelius (in 251 A.D.) had appointed an exorcist to each region, in all probability to deal with such cases.

In contemporary times in Britain, the Bishop of Southwark, Dr. Mervyn Stockwood, has appointed another bishop to be his official exorcist. Bishop Markham is the first bishop to have this role, and he regards his job as being a consultant, helping priests "with what should be regarded as part of the whole caring ministry of the Church." He wants to be regarded as "a spiritual counsellor in a pastoral sphere." There is, however, a serious divergence of opinion in the Church of England concerning exorcism, and some years ago a commission was set up, headed by the then Bishop of Exeter, Dr. Robert C. Mortimer. The commission recommended that bishops appoint their own trained exorcists to expel evil forces from people and places. It had no doubts that evil forces were at work but stressed that all possible medical and psychological explanations should first be thoroughly investigated before any attempt was made to exorcise. Training centers for potential exorcists were also suggested.

Two years after the findings of this commission there occurred a horrific case in Yorkshire where a man killed his wife after undergoing an all-night ceremony of exorcism in a church vestry, conducted by a vicar and a Methodist minister. Altogether some fifty evil spirits were alleged to have been expelled. But some remained—or alternatively the man's mental illness was sharpened by the histrionics and apparent credibility of the service. As a result of this very savage murder, there was a tremendous outcry, involving a group of sixty-five prominent theologians and academicians, pointing out that the Church was in danger of making a serious error of judgment by giving official status to exorcism. They also called on the Archbishops of Canterbury and York to ensure that the practice received no official encouragement nor received any official status. However, the primates made it quite clear that there was a continuing place, with strict safeguards, for exorcism in modern times.

Dom Robert Petitpierre, O.S.B., underlines this, writing in his book *Exorcism*. He says:

> In Western countries today, the widespread apostasy from the Christian faith, accompanied by an increasing recourse to black magic and occult practises, is revealing the presence and the power of evil forces. . . . The need, therefore, for the restoration of the practise of exorcism to its proper place is becoming steadily more urgent and more evident.

But what is exorcism's proper place? Obviously if handled ineptly the healing ceremony is highly dangerous. The emotions of patient and exorcist can be played upon so much that they can become inextricably tangled, and their minds can then begin to fall apart with rapid acceleration. There are many examples of imagined demonic attack, but a disturbing number of well-accredited cases when the victim has shown every sign of suddenly having powers that he or she never had before.

Symptoms of acute demonic attack, as listed by some exorcists and theologians, begin with a change of personality both in terms of intelligence and character. Various physical changes seem to occur, although these vary from case to case. The most classical are heightened strength, convulsions, catatonic symptoms, falling, clouding of the consciousness, anesthesia to pain and changed voice. The mental changes include preternatural knowledge, clairvoyance, telepathy, prediction and other occult powers as well as the understanding of previously unknown languages. The spiritual changes are basically a strong reactive fear to Christ, considerable blasphemy and an abhorrence of prayer. Both the physical and mental changes are scientifically inexplicable in this collective form.

One of the most powerful descriptions of the horrors of possession comes in Sir Edward B. Tyler's *Primitive Culture*, published in London in 1871:

> . . . the mysterious unseen Power throws him helpless on the ground, jerks and writhes him in convulsions, makes him leap upon the bystanders with a giant's strength and a wild beast's ferocity, impels him, with distorted face and frantic gesture, and voice not his own or seemingly human, to pour forth wild incoherent ravings, or with thought and eloquence beyond his sober faculties to command, to counsel, to foretell—such a one seems to those who watch him, and even to himself, to have become the mere instrument of a spirit which has seized him or entered into him, a possessing demon in whose personality the patient believes so implicity that he often imagines a personal name for it, which it can declare when it speaks in its own voice and character through his organs of speech; at last, quitting the medium's spent and jaded body, the intruding spirit departs as it came.

The Roman Catholic Church, unlike the Church of England, has not revised its policy concerning exorcism, and it retains its exorcism rite which was originally issued in 1619 and called the *Rituale Romanum*. It is a very interesting and in many ways enlightened document and is in no way a mere series of outdated incantations. It is also worth analyzing in some detail, taking the ritual section by section.

Initially, the first point of the ritual ensures that the

priest is both mature, pious and objective. Considering how many priests have used the process of exorcism to their own subjective advantage through the centuries, this is a very necessary precaution.

1.–A priest—one who is expressly and in special wise authorized by the Ordinary—when he intends to perform an exorcism over persons tormented by the devil, must be properly distinguished for his piety, prudence, and integrity of life. He should fulfil this devout undertaking in all constancy and humility, being utterly immune to any striving for human aggrandizement, and relying not on his own, but on the divine power. Morover, he ought to be of mature years, and revered not alone for his office but for his moral qualities.

Study, too, is important and past precedents are very necessary.

2.–In order to exercise his ministry rightly, he should resort to a great deal more study of the matter (which has to be passed over here for sake of brevity) by examining approved authors and cases from experience; on the other hand, let him carefully observe the few more important points enumerated here.

Naivete is important to avoid and the authorities make it absolutely clear that possession by evil spirits is not a run-of-the-mill event.

3.–Especially, he should not believe too readily that a person is possessed by an evil spirit; but he ought to ascertain the signs by which a person possessed can be distinguished from one who is suffering from melancholy or some other illness. Signs of possession are the following: ability to speak with some facility in a strange tongue or to understand it when spoken by another; the faculty of divulging future and hidden events; display of powers which are beyond the subject's age and natural condition; and various other indications which, when taken together as a whole, pile up the evidence.

If the patient is possessed, then it is important to find the quickest and most forceful method of despatching the demon.

4.–In order to understand these matters better, let him inquire of the person possessed, following upon one or the other act of exorcism, what the latter experienced in his body or soul while the exorcism was being performed, and to learn also what particular words in the form had a more intimidating effect upon the devil, so that hereafter these words may be employed with greater stress and frequency.

The exorcist also has to be prepared for the evil spirit to be highly divisive. He also has to prepare himself for a long-drawn-out battle.

5.–He will be on his guard against the arts and subterfuges which the evil spirits are wont to use in deceiving the exorcist. For often-times they give deceptive answers and make it difficult to understand them, so that the exorcist might tire and give up, or so it might appear that the afflicted one is in no wise possessed by the devil.

Even at the point of deliverance the demon could still be cunning and any complacency on the part of the exorcist could well be disastrous.

6.–Once in a while, after they are already recognized, they conceal themselves and leave the body practically free from every molestation, so that the victim believes himself completely delivered. Yet the exorcist may not desist until he sees the signs of deliverance.

The patient is not to be seen as cooperative and would battle the exorcist as hard as the evil spirit inside him can push him.

7.–At times, moreover, the evil spirits place whatever obstacles they can in the way, so that the patient may not submit to exorcism, or they try to convince him that his affliction is a natural one. Meanwhile, during the exorcism they cause him to fall asleep, and dangle some illusion before him, while they seclude themselves, so that the afflicted one appears to be freed.

No one else but an ordained priest can exorcise, and recourse to magicians is taboo.

8.–Some reveal a crime which has been committed and the perpetrators thereof, as well as the means of putting an end to it. Yet the afflicted person must beware of having recourse on this account to sorcerers or necromancers or to any parties except the ministers of the Church, or of making use of any superstition, nay any sort of forbidden practice.

The evil spirit might also absent himself for periods, thus allowing another area of deception to occur.

9.–Sometimes the devil will leave the possessed person in peace and even allow him to receive the Holy Eucharist, to make it appear that he has departed. In fact, the arts and frauds of the evil one for deceiving a man are innumerable. For this reason the exorcist must be on his guard, lest he fall into this trap.

Evil spirits are of variable strength and for the hard-liners a special technique has to be used.

10.–Wherefore, he will be mindful of the words of our Lord (Matt. 17:20) to the effect that there is a certain type of evil spirit who cannot be driven out except by prayer and fasting. Therefore, let him avail himself of these two means above all for imploring the divine assistance in expelling demons, after the example of the holy fathers; and not only himself, but let him induce others, so far as possible, to do the same.

The ideal place for an exorcism to take place is consecrated ground where the evil spirit is far from at home. The most dangerous place to exorcise is outside holy places.

11.–If it can be done conveniently, the possessed person should be led to church or to some other sacred and worthy place where the exorcism will be held, away from the crowd. But if the person is ill, or for any valid reason, the exorcism may take place in a private home.

Despite the presence of the evil spirit, the patient has to be surrounded by holy ritual.

12.–The subject, if in good mental and physical health, should be exhorted to implore God's help, to fast, and to fortify himself by frequent reception of penance and Holy Communion, at the discretion of the priest. And in the course of the exorcism he should be fully recollected, with his intention fixed on God, Whom he should entreat with firm faith and in all humility. And if he is all the more grievously tormented, he ought to bear this patiently, never doubting the divine assistance.

Artifacts are important, particularly in the case of the crucifix. This serves to protect the exorcist as well as the possessed.

13.–He ought to have a crucifix at hand or somewhere in sight. If relics of the saints are available, they are to be applied in a reverent way to the breast or the head of the person possessed (the relics must be properly and securely encased and covered). One will see to it that these sacred objects are not treated improperly or that no injury is done them by the evil spirit. However, one should not hold the Holy Eucharist over the head of the person nor in any way apply It to his body, owing to the danger of desecration.

The exorcist is not allowed to pry into the private affairs of the patient nor is he expected to ask spurious questions.

14.–The exorcist must not digress into senseless prattle nor ask superfluous questions or such as are prompted by curiosity, particularly if they pertain to future and hidden matters, all of which have nothing to do with his office. Instead, he will bid the unclean spirit keep silence and answer only when asked. Neither ought he to give any credence to the devil if the latter maintains that he is the spirit of some saint or of a deceased party, or even claims to be a good angel.

Only the relevant questions were required. The exorcist also has to be on guard against sardonic remarks by the evil spirit. He should particularly prevent any jocular reaction to these comments from those attending the exorcism.

15.–But necessary questions are, for example: about the number and name of the spirits inhabiting the patient, about the time when they entered into him, the cause thereof, and such like. As for all jesting, laughing, and nonsense on the part of the evil spirit—the exorcist should prevent it or contemn it, and he will exhort the bystanders (whose number must be very limited) to pay no attention to such goings on; neither are they to put any question on the subject. Rather they should intercede for him to God in all humility and urgency.

It is essential that the priest be confident and authoritarian at all times. At all costs the evil spirit must not find his opponent inferior in any way.

16.–Let the priest pronounce the exorcisms in a commanding and authoritative voice, and at the same time with great confidence, humility, and fervor; and when he sees that the spirit is sorely vexed, then he oppresses and threatens all the more. If he notices that the person afflicted is experiencing a disturbance in some part of his body or an acute pain or a swelling appears in some part, he traces the sign of the Cross over that place and sprinkles it with holy water, which he must have at hand for this purpose.

Each case is different, as is each evil spirit. Therefore it is important for the exorcist to gauge the strengths and weaknesses of the demon as exactly as possible.

17.–He will pay attention as to what words in particular cause the evil spirits to tremble, repeating them the more frequently. And when he comes to a threatening expression, he recurs to it again and again, always increasing the punishment. If he perceives that he is making progress, let him persist for two, three, four hours, and longer if he can, until victory is attained.

The ritual makes it very clear that there should be no overstepping by the exorcist into the territory of the physician.

18.–The exorcist should guard against giving or recommending any medicine to the patient, but should leave this care to physicians.

The exorcist is warned to be extremely careful when attempting to expel evil spirits from women. Other women of known repute should be in attendance just in case the exorcist is himself overcome with evil thoughts.

19.–While performing the exorcism over a woman, he ought always to have assisting him several women of good repute, who will hold on to the person when she is harassed by the evil spirit. These assistants ought if possible to be close relatives of the subject, and for the sake of decency the exorcist will avoid saying or doing anything which might prove an occasion of evil thoughts to himself or to the others.

It is essential to exhort answers to certain questions from the evil spirit.

20.–During the exorcism he shall preferably employ words from Holy Writ, rather than forms of his own or of someone else. He shall, moreover, command the devil to tell whether he is detained in that body by necromancy, by evil signs or amulets; and if the one possessed has taken the latter by mouth, he should be made to vomit them; if he has them concealed on his person, he should expose them; and when discovered they must be burned. Moreover, the person should be exhorted to reveal all his temptations to the exorcist.

Should deliverance be achieved it is vital that the patient be warned to protect himself carefully against further attack.

21.–Finally, after the possessed one has been freed, let him be admonished to guard himself carefully against falling into sin, so as to afford no opportunity to the evil spirit of returning, lest the last state of that man become worse than the former.

Obviously some parts of the ritual are very outdated but the majority of it is straightforward and unhysterical.

But some priests believe exorcism is also a calming influence on "false" possession. The Reverend Robert Mortimer, formerly Bishop of Exeter, stated in an interview with Richard Deutch, "Disturbances of this sort often are purely subjective. Yet the rite of exorcism often seems to quiet the person's mind." Nevertheless, Mortimer, like Israel, is utterly convinced that demons really exist outside the human mind.

The apparent psychic attack has been well recorded by a victim who wishes to remain anonymous and who claimed to have written down this account without realizing she had done so. It is in the possession of Richard Deutch and reads:

> An icy stillness seemed to creep over the room. It felt as if suddenly a powerful blow had been dealt to the stomach, and the chair in the corner of the room seemed to be going quite mad. Dancing, almost, but moving about certainly.
>
> Can you feel colour? The hue of cold seemed to pervade the room. The coldness departed as mysteriously as it had come, but some minutes later it returned, but it felt differently, an inquiring atmosphere, rather than icy stillness. The coldness passed through the house and then departed for the night.
>
> The coldness is difficult to describe, because it is not one that comes of snow or wind, but rather of a temperatureless presence that seems to take hold of the abstract part of yourself. The experience is always of the unexplainable, relying on feel, atmosphere and instinct. This is sometimes the only "physical" evidence one has of psychic attack; more often the whole operation is based on mental attitude. Here "feel" and "instinct" play an even bigger part and it is of course even more difficult to explain or rationalize—even to yourself.

The Reverend Canon (Emeritus) John D. Pearce-Higgins gives strong support to Dr. Martin Israel's opinion that possession is most likely to be imposed on the victim by someone who was close to him or her when alive.

Pearce-Higgins is a founder member of The Church's Fellowship for Psychical and Spiritual Studies. He visited a daughter who had been disinherited by a wealthy mother. Shortly after the mother's death there was considerable poltergeist activity and footsteps were heard. The daughter seemed possessed by the mother, went into trance and on one occasion attacked her husband with a hammer. Needless to say there had been little love lost between husband and mother-in-law when she had been alive. Gradually, however, through prayer, conciliation was attained.

Pearce-Higgins feels that there *is* a demonic element in man and quotes C. S. Lewis's words when, asked if he believed in devils, said, "Yes, I know lots of us." He also considers that there is little need for an exorcism in case of earthbound possessive spirits—and they therefore, in most cases, only require a Requiem. By this he implies that exorcism should be reserved for demonry. Equally he feels that dabbling in the occult *causes* possession and he writes concerning Blatty's situation in *The Exorcist:*

> The whole trouble (which was supposed to be based on a real case) was started by use of a Ouija board. Once again I cannot too strongly stress how dangerous any dabbling with the occult is, and how right the Church has been to discountenance any but specialists indulging in these studies.

Pearce-Higgins finds that the entities that need expelling are of extremely low intelligence—one hardly knows indeed whether they are not "elemental" subhuman creatures who require to be restrained or restricted before they can be rescued. For this purpose I have been forced to use a prayer of exorcism in the more traditional sense, condemning them after due warning into outer darkness "until the day of repentance."

Pearce-Higgins believes that demons are fallen angels and "there is certainly in the gospel a sternness in dealing with such spiritual forces, in the words of Christ, which justifies us in binding them first so that they can do no more damage, just as we have to keep dangerous characters in custody." But he still takes the Israel view that even these lowly demons must in the end be reconciled and brought to God.

Other cases of possession in the twentieth century have been many and varied and I am only including the most well authenticated here. But before I do this, I thought it worthwhile to go back to 1865, when a very carefully detailed case history of possession was made by a German Jesuit, Father Adolf Rodewyk in *Die dämonische Besessenheit*. Rodewyk's thesis was to conciliate his Church's traditional judgments, in the light of the *Rituale Romanum*, with new scientific findings that ranged from medicine and psychiatry to parapsychology. The following startling and demonic account is one of the very first "scientific" cases of possession and was the forerunner to many such descriptions of twentieth-century cases. The victims were two brothers, Theobald and Josef, who became possessed in the German town of Illfurt. The possession began in 1865 and lasted four years. The Church authorities of the time, notes Father Rodewyk, judged them as truly possessed in the light of the *Rituale Romanum*. But Rodewyk's problem was, having taken the outward evidence as reliable, could he judge them as truly possessed in the light of present-day knowledge?

The boys became possessed when Theobald was ten and Josef eight. During their years of possession they were mainly confined to bed and at least two or three times a day they intertwined their legs in such a way that they could not be separated. They also stood on their heads and legs with the remainder of their bodies raised high. The parish record states: "no external pressure could restore their bodies to a natural position until the Devil was willing to leave his victims in peace."

The parish records revealed a wealth of interesting information, although they are the only substantiation of the "evidence." The boys, apparently, would turn their faces to the walls and paint demonic faces on it, with whom they afterward talked and played. Each boy also apparently levitated and the records say:

While sitting on a chair, boy and chair were at times lifted into the air, and then dropped in such a way that the boy was flung into one corner of the room and the chair into the opposite corner. Even the mother, when sitting on the child's bed, might be lifted into the air and hurled into a corner, although without any damage.

The bodies of the boys swelled, and they expelled foam, feathers and seaweed. Often the children were "covered with feathers that gave off a disgusting odour." While asleep, the boys apparently still obeyed their black master, and if a rosary was placed anywhere near them they would cower under the coverlets until it was removed. Unheated by a stove, the room was unbearably hot, although this great heat was reduced by the sprinking of holy water. On their rare expeditions outside, the boys climbed trees with the agility of cats and were able to sit "on the thinnest branches, which never broke under them." The curtains were often pulled down as if by invisible hands and the windows burst open with "incredible speed, entirely by themselves." There was also considerable poltergeist phenomena.

The appearance of any priest or deeply religious figure in the house would cause the possessed boys to crawl under the furniture, or, in extremes, to jump out the window. But the appearance of a "mediocre Christian" would cause the boys to show "great delight" and to cry out triumphantly, "This is one of ours. They should all be like that." But it is just this sort of comment that makes this part of the parish records suspect, for it can be seen how the blanket description of "possession" can easily be turned to religious propaganda purposes.

Eventually exorcism took place, although it would appear that the only detail relates to Theobald. The parish records of Illfurt state that he was taken to an "institution" in nearby Schiltigheim where the "devil was silent for three days." Finally, on the fourth day a voice shrieked, "Here I am, and I am in a fury." The nun on duty then said, "Who are you?" and the reply came, "I am the Lord of Darkness." The voice reminded the nun of "a calf being strangled." Other factors emerged during the exorcism. Theobald recognised no one, including his mother, and he was so violent that he had to be bound. He could detect religious artifacts, even when secretly sewn into his clothing, and he was so deaf that he was unable to hear a pistol fired close to his ear. Both boys were also apparently able to converse freely in French, Latin and English, as well as understanding some French and Spanish dialects. Previous to their possession, they could speak only German, their mother tongue.

The Illfurt boys are a classic case of possession. It must be remembered that the other reasons for their behavior are numerous—mental illness, epilepsy, reaction against a deeply pious background and so on. It is also a little too much of a coincidence that cases of possession are more often than not recorded in the midst of a deeply religious community. Nuns, for instance, seem particularly prone to possession. Telepathy is another factor that could be linked with the foreign languages of the Illfurt case. But even so, if the Illfurt boys were mentally ill, telepathic

and epileptic—and overall they were immaturely rebel-
ling against an overtly pious background —there remains
a good deal to be explained in this case. Or were the other
details mere theatrical illustrations of possession written
up in the parish records for religious propaganda purposes?

One of the most renowned cases of exorcism took
place in Iowa in 1928. A member of the Capuchin order,
the Reverend Theophilus Riesinger, persuaded his Catholic authorities to let him exorcise a highly religious,
forty-year-old woman who was possessed by an evil spirit
that forbade her to go to church or experience any religious feeling and put thoughts into her head of which she
was deeply ashamed. Once in the convent where Riesinger proposed to carry out the exorcism, she became en-
raged and violent. En route to the convent Riesinger
found that his car was mysteriously slowed down and
when food was sprinkled with holy water, the patient
threw it out of the window. It is important to add that the
patient had no knowledge of the presence of the holy water.

Aware that he was in acute danger, Riesinger took care
to guard himself spiritually all the time. This protection
included constant prayer while driving. Eventually the
woman was placed upon a mattress, her arms tightly
bound, and the exorcism commenced. As Riesinger began the ritual, the woman, despite her bonds and a battery of the strongest nuns, rose from the bed, landed high
above the door and clung to the wall. She was pulled
down with difficulty. As the exorcism resumed, a loud,
shrill voice filled the room as if in pain. It was definitely
not at all like the voice of the patient. Attracted by the
noise, a crowd formed around the walls of the convent
while the evil spirit continued to howl. Various voices
emanated from the woman, some of which were alarm-

ingly gutteral and bestial. Animal noises were also produced, including those of lions, hyenas, dogs, cats and
cattle. Sometimes these came separately, at other times
together. Then a dialogue began, some of which is reproduced below:

EXORCIST: In the name of Jesus and His most Blessed
Mother, Mary the Immaculate, who crushed the head of
the serpent: Tell me the truth. Who is the leader or
prince among you? What is your name?

DEVIL (barking like the hound of hell): Beelzebub.

EXORCIST: You call yourself Beelzebub. Are you not Lucifer, the prince of the devils?

DEVIL: No, not the prince, the chieftain, but one of the
leaders.

EXORCIST: You were therefore not a human being, but
you are one of the fallen angels, who with selfish pride
wanted to be like unto God?

DEVIL (with grinning teeth): Yes, that is so. Ha, how we
hate him!

EXORCIST: Why are you called Beelzebub if you are not
the prince of the devils?

DEVIL: Enough, my name is Beelzebub.

EXORCIST: From the point of influence and dignity you
must rank near Lucifer, or do you hail from the lower
choir of angels?

DEVIL: I once belonged to the seraphic choir.

EXORCIST: What would you do if God made it possible
for you to atone for your injustice to Him?

DEVIL (demonic sneering): Are you a competent theolo-
gian?

EXORCIST: How long have you been torturing this poor
woman?

DEVIL: Since her fourteenth year.

EXORCIST: How dared you enter into that innocent girl and torture her like that?

DEVIL (sneeringly): Ha, did not her own father curse us into her?

EXORCIST: By why did you, Beelzebub, alone take possession of her? Who gave you that permission?

DEVIL: Don't talk so foolishly. Don't I have to render obedience to Satan?

EXORCIST: Then you are here at the direction and command of Lucifer?

DEVIL: Well, how could it be otherwise?

Realizing that he had the Prince of Darkness on his hands rather than a mere demon, Riesinger addressed him in English, German and Latin. Once he misheard the Devil and was sternly rebuked. Then the Devil stated that the patient had been cursed by her father because he had been demonically influenced ever since he had been damned. Riesinger than said:

EXORCIST: Then I solemnly command you in the name of the Crucified Saviour of Nazareth that you present the father of this woman and that he give me the answer.

(A deeper, rougher voice replied which had been sometimes noticed alongside the voice of the Devil.)

EXORCIST: Are you the unfortunate father who has cursed his own child?

VOICE: No.

EXORCIST: Who are you then?

VOICE: I am Judas.

EXORCIST: What, Judas! Are you Judas Iscariot, the former Apostle?

VOICE: Yes, I am the one.

The patient then began to spit and vomit. Then—

191

EXORCIST: What business have you here?

VOICE: To bring her to despair, so that she would commit suicide and hang herself! She must get the rope, she must go to hell.

Finally the spirit of the dead father spoke, admitting to unsuccessfully attempting to make his daughter commit incest with him. He had cursed her because of her resistance. The exorcism continued and so did the howls of the Devil. Religious relics were brought into the battle and the following prayer used. Apparently the Devil found the words, and particularly the mention of his old archenemy St. Michael, quite unbearable.

Saint Michael the Archangel, defend us in battle. Be our safeguard against the wickedness and destruction of the Devil. Restrain him O God, we humbly beseech Thee, and do thou, O Prince of the heavenly host, by the power of God cast him into hell with the other evil spirits, who prowl about the world seeking the ruin of souls. Amen.

Now facing eventual defeat, the Devil threatened everyone in attendance at the exorcism, but particularly Riesinger. Despite renewed prayers on his car journey, he blacked out on a bridge and wrecked his car. Miraculously he came out of the smashed vehicle alive. When he returned to the convent, roars of laughter greeted him from the patient. When he had laughed his fill, the Devil told Riesinger that St. Michael had saved him from being crushed to death.

Eventually it became clear that four spirits were possessing the woman—Satan; Judas Iscariot; her father, Jacob; and Mina, Jacob's lover. The last turned out to be a child-murderer. But after a twenty-three-day exorcism and the near collapse of Riesinger, the spirits were successfully exorcised from the woman and she returned to complete normality.

Despite the theatricality of this account, it is extremely well documented and much witnessed. Father Theophilus Riesinger was an accepted exorcist and this account was taken from the booklet *Begone Satan!* originally published in German by the Reverend Vogl and later translated and republished by the Reverend Celestine Kapsner of St. John's Abbey, Collegeville, Minnesota.

In the early 1930s a psychiatrist who was also a convinced Catholic, Dr. Jean Lhermitte, wrote:

> It must be admitted that the science of psychiatry takes a very humble place amongst the other biological disciplines, for psychiatry operates on a plane where body and soul meet, and we still do not know how that "seam of soul and body" is made.

Dr. Lhermitte points out that the great epidemics of possession raged when psychiatry had largely not come into being and that, unknown to doctor or priest, a combination of illness and autosuggestion was often present under the guise of possession. Lhermitte then chose a typical case—that of a sexually confused young nun who was unwisely told by her superiors that she was "possessed by devils." In archetypical manner she would "throw herself into a thousand contorted attitudes and gave way to the wildest and most fantastic tricks. Worse still, in between the periods of exorcism she began to smash things and utter prophecies, so that the peace and recollection of the convent were exceedingly disturbed." Even more typically (reminiscent of religious fervor in African tribal possession) the nun tore off her wimple, shouted obscenities to all and sundry and proceeded to "twirl and dance and to assume innumerable fantastic postures." The unfortunate nun was eventually "cured of demonic possession" by electric shock treatment. However, Dr. Lhermitte does not reject true possession—he merely regards many cases as hysterical, derivative possession— "demonopathy"—where the patient imitates the phenomena of true demonic possession.

Dr. W. Grey Walter runs the Burden Neurological Institute in Bristol, England. There, he is a pioneer in a technique in which minute electrodes are planted in the brain. Through these electrodes the brain receives very small charges of electricity. So tiny are the electrodes that a considerable quantity can be implanted simultaneously in the brain. There is no pain involved and the treatment can be retained from one period to another by the patient wearing a beretlike headcover while staying at the institute. Dr. Walter claims to be able to cure possession by making small holes in the "supraorbital white matter in anxiety patients and in the paracingulate region of the compulsive obsessional patient." After twenty years in the field Dr. Walter claims to be able to anticipate, with a high degree of accuracy, which brain areas are the initiation of specific fears and images. He relates the supraorbital region of the brain to the generation of fear, and states," If you make a little lesion here it is almost like a lobotomy in its effect on symptoms, but the lesion is minute and has no side effects." Also, by "causing a lesion in the paracingulate region, compulsive patients are relieved as dramatically and can function normally in their jobs."

An earlier and less credible scientist, Dr. Carl A. Wickland, functioned in the mid-thirties. Dr. Wickland's apparatus is best explained by himself in 1935:

The static machine which I use, constructed by myself under the direction of intelligent spiritual forces, is made according to the Wimhurst pattern and contains fourteen thirty-inch-diameter glass discs, all active, giving a powerful current.

Dr. Wickland was a member of the Chicago and Illinois state medical societies as well as the American Society for the Advancement of Science. One of his supporters is Canon J. D. Pearse-Higgins, who writes:

> A good many patients in mental hospitals suffering from hallucinations, hearing or speaking in strange voices, or suffering from split-personalities, *may* be cases of possession who would benefit from treatment similar to that given by Dr. Wickland.

Pearce-Higgins claimed that Wickland played a light *external* electric current along the spine or over the head of the possessed person, which made the possessing spirit hurriedly depart and enter into the body of Wickland's medium wife, Anna. Through Anna, states Pearce-Higgins, the possessing spirit could be cross-examined.

It must be pointed out that many of Wickland's spirit transfers were not of a highly demonic nature but were more likely to be the earthbound spirits of loved ones, relations or the rootless. What is more, most of his possessing spirits took some time to realize that they were actually in command of another person's body or that they had transferred to his wife's body. Wickland wrote:

> Those intelligences whose reasoning faculties are alert can generally be made to realise that their situation is unusual when attention is called to the dissimilarity between their former bodily features, hands, feet, as well as clothes, and those of the psychic. This is especially so when the spirit is a man, for the difference will then be more readily no-

ticed. Following the statement that the body which is being controlled belongs to my wife, spirits usually retort: "I am not your wife," and great deal of explanation is required before they can be brought to recognition of the fact that they are in temporary possession of another's body.

Wickland strongly rejected any question of fraud and firmly states that

foreign languages totally unknown to Mrs. Wickland are spoken, expressions never heard by her are used, while the identity of the controlling spirits has again and again been verified and corroborations innumerable have been made.

That may be so, but very little evidence has remained to support Dr. Wickland's theories and although Canon Pearce-Higgins has repeatedly asked for such material from people who knew Wickland and his work well, nothing has been forthcoming. Nevertheless Wickland is one of the few exorcists who have purportedly taped a dialogue between himself and a possessing spirit and this is reproduced below. It is exceptional in the mundanity of the conversation and the indignation of the spirit concerned. Wickland is talking to the spirit of Carrie Huntington, who he believed to be possessing one of his patients—a Mrs. Burton.

DR. WICKLAND: Tell us who you are.
SPIRIT: I do not wish you to hold my hands.
DOCTOR: You must sit still.
SPIRIT: Why do you treat me like this?
DOCTOR: Who are you?
SPIRIT: Why do you want to know?

DOCTOR: You have come here as a stranger, and we would like to know who you are.

SPIRIT: What are you so interested for?

DOCTOR: We should like to know with whom we are associated. If a stranger came to your home, would you not like to know his name?

SPIRIT: I do not want to be here and I do not know any of you. Somebody pushed me in here and I do not think it is right to force me in like that. When I came in and sat down on the chair you grabbed my hands as if I were a prisoner. Why was I pushed in here?

DOCTOR: You were probably in the dark.

SPIRIT: It seems somebody took me by force. [Dr. Wickland's explanation is that "guiding intelligences" in the spirit world forced such possessing spirits to communicate through his wife, so that they might gain understanding.]

DOCTOR: Was there any reason for it?

SPIRIT: I do not know of any reason, and I do not see why I should be bothered like that.

DOCTOR: Was no reason given for handling you in this manner?

SPIRIT: It has been a terrible time for me for quite a while. I have been tormented to death. I have been driven here, there, and everywhere. I am getting so provoked about it that I feel like giving everything a good shaking.

DOCTOR: What have they done to you?

SPIRIT: It seems too terrible. If I walk around, I am so very miserable. I do not know what it is. Sometimes it seems as if my senses were being knocked out of me. Something comes on me like thunder and lightning. It makes such a noise. This terrible noise—it is awful! I cannot stand it any more, and I will not either! [This comment, according to Dr. Wickland, refers to the spir-

197

it's impressions of, and reaction to, the treatment with static electricity.]

DOCTOR: We shall be glad if you will not stand it any more.

SPIRIT: Am I not welcome? And if I am not, I do not care!

DOCTOR: You are not very particular.

SPIRIT: I have had so much hardship.

DOCTOR: How long have you been dead?

SPIRIT: Why do you speak that way? I am not dead. I am as alive as I can be, and I feel as if I were young again.

DOCTOR: Have you not felt, at times, as if you were somebody else?

SPIRIT: At times I feel very strange, especially when it knocks me senseless. I feel very bad. I do not feel that I should have this suffering. I do not know why I should have such things.

DOCTOR: Probably it is necessary.

SPIRIT: I feel I should be free to go where I please, but it seems I have no will of my own anymore. I try, but it seems somebody else takes possession of me and gets me into some place where they knock me nearly senseless. If I knew it, I would never go there, but there is a person who seems to have the right to take me everywhere; I feel I should have the right to take her. [This, according to Dr. Wickland, refers to the possessing spirit's relation with his patient, Mrs. Burton.]

DOCTOR: What business have you with her? Can't you live your own life?

SPIRIT: I live my own life, but she interferes with me. I talk to her. She wants to chase me out. I feel like chasing her out, and that is a real struggle. I cannot see why I should not have the right just as well as she has.

DOCTOR: Probably you are interfering with her.

SPIRIT: She wants to get rid of me. I am not bothering her. I only talk to her sometimes.

DOCTOR: Does she know you talk to her?

SPIRIT: Sometimes she does, and then she chases me right out. She acts all right, but she gets so provoked. Then, when she gets into that place, I am knocked senseless and I feel terrible. I have no power to take her away. She makes me get out.

DOCTOR: You should not stay around her.

SPIRIT: It is my body, it is not hers. She has no right there. I do not see why she interferes with me.

DOCTOR: She interferes with your selfishness.

SPIRIT: I feel I have some right in life—I think so.

DOCTOR: You passed out of your body without understanding the fact, and have been bothering the lady. You should go to the spirit world and not hover around her.

SPIRIT: You say I am hovering around. I am not hovering around, and I am not one to interfere, but I want a little to say about things.

DOCTOR: That is why you had the "thunder" and the "knocks."

SPIRIT: That was all right for a while, but lately it is terrible. I must have understanding.

DOCTOR: You will have it now.

SPIRIT: I will do anything to stop that terrible knocking.

Possession has been seen through a number of mediums such as the Ouija board, spiritualism, witchcraft, satanism and black magic. Therefore its manifestations are very diverse. Medically speaking, it has also been seen in epilepsy, schizophrenia and hysteria. Once again its diversity is immense. The following case histories of possession tend to pinpoint this very wide spectrum.

From the religious point of view, a Texas minister reported on one of his possessed flock in the early 1970s.

> During my stay we ministered deliverance in Jack's home to a young man named Jim. One evil spirit proved most stubborn. Its name was "insanity" and it screamed and raged and swore. As we gave the repeated commands for the demon to come out, Jim fell on the floor and began to retch. All at once he brought up a quantity of mucouslike material. While Jack Herd's poor wife cleaned up the mess on the rug in one spot, Jim continued to be sick in another. Then to our shock and dismay, Jim lunged free from our grasp, thrust his face directly into the vomit and began to eat it. As we dragged him away, the demon within him began to scream: "Leave me alone! . . . "

On the opposite pole an Anglican priest was asked to exorcise a schizophrenic by a psychiatrist who was unable to make any progress with his patient at all:

> She . . . did not respond to any known hospital treatment. He was convinced that she was possessed. At this time I had jumped on the passing theological band-wagon of the time and had firmly demythologised everything in sight—including the devil and all his minions. I declined the invitation to join in this particular ministration and somewhat presumptuously suggested further medical treatment. This was sufficient to invoke from him the challenge. "Were you or were you not, in your ordination, given authority to bind and loose? Here is a woman who is bound—loose her!" [During the ser-

vice] . . . At the word of command that the binding
spirit should leave her in the Name of Jesus, there
was a great cry which came from her, "Leave us
alone." All very biblical. She remembered nothing of
this afterwards. . . .

As to the power of holy artifacts, Professor T. K. Oster-
reich has this to say of one such case:

> As soon as the boy had to pass a church cru-
> cifix . . . he fell unconscious to the earth. At the
> exorcism in church . . . the possessed uttered a ter-
> rible cry. We seemed no longer to hear a human
> voice but that of a savage animal, and so powerful
> that the howlings . . . were heard at a distance of
> several hundred metres from the convent chap-
> el. . . . The weak child flung the strong father to
> earth with such violence that our hearts were in our
> mouths. At length after a long struggle he was over-
> come By his father, the men who were witnesses and
> one lay brother, and led into the presbytery. By way
> of precaution we had him bound hand and foot with
> straps, but he moved his limbs as if nothing of the
> kind had been done.

Father John Richards, an Anglican priest who has written an introduction to what he calls the "demonic dimension in pastoral care," sees false possession as just as
great a danger as true, demonic possession. He lists the
causes, in both cases, as follows:

1. *False Possession* (but in no way implying "unreal")
   (a) *Psychogenic* (i.e., originating in the mind)
      (i) By suggestion

    (ii) By autosuggestion

    (iii) By projection—whether self-induced or by
          another

    (iv) Delusion

    (v) Passivity phenomena—where the patient
          states that his thoughts, feelings, speech and
          actions are not his own

(b) *Medical*—Symptomatic epilepsy, etc.

(c) *By Living Person(s)*

    (i) Relations

    (ii) Occult manipulation

(d) *By Earth-Bound Spirits*

2. *True (Demonic) Possession*

(a) Due to

    (i) Accident, e.g., heredity, place, occult experi-
        ence and healing, occult transference and
        curses

    (ii) Invitation knowingly, e.g., Devil subscrip-
        tion

    (iii) Invitation unknowingly, e.g., mediums

(b) By

    (i) Demon

    (ii) Demons

(c) Degree:

    (i) Partial/"Lucid"/ "external demonopathy"

    (ii) Complete/"Somnambulistic"/"internal demo-
        nopathy"

Dr. Lechler in Part II of Kurt Koch's *Occult Bondage and Deliverance* has produced some of the few existing pieces of diagnostic writing concerning possession:

    1. . . . a possessed person, though he may be restless and even driven into a rage at times, will nevertheless remain sane in his thoughts.

2. While the mental patient will speak in extravagant tones of the demons he alleges to be living inside himself, the possessed person avoids all mention of demons as long as no one approaches him on a spiritual level.

3. The voices which a patient says originate from strange people . . . are . . . usually . . . of a pathological nature. . . . The satanic voices heard by a possessed person are of a completely different nature. . . . In general then, if the voices are demonic in origin they will attempt to lure the person away from God, whereas if they are the result of some mental abnormality they will speak of unnatural and nonsensical things.

4. Experience shows that in the case of schizophrenics, a person who continually talks about being possessed is in fact deluding himself. On the contrary a person who is really possessed will never let the idea of possession enter his head, even if there is no other explanation for his condition.

5. . . . if blasphemous thoughts arise in a person's heart and are consciously expressed without the slightest remorse, they will in almost every case be promoted by the devil. On the other hand, if thoughts force themselves upon a person, and instead of being expressed are abhorred and genuinely repented of, they will most likely be of a pathological nature. A demonically affected person will care little about blasphemous thoughts, but the mental depressive will lament the fact that he thinks such things.

A case of possession revealed by automatic writing was claimed just before the war by Doctors Milton H. Erickson and Lawrence S. Kubie in a paper in *The Psychoanalytic Quarterly* 8 No. 4 entitled "The Permanent

Relief of an Obsessional Phobia by Means of Communications with an Unsuspected Dual Personality." Their patient, Miss Damon, was suffering from obsessive fears about leaving doors open and an intense hatred of cats. Putting her under hypnosis, Erickson and Kubie found her first trance was characterized by "a marked degree of amnesia, ready hand levitation and profound catalepsy." Later she tried automatic writing, a process which revealed her "other" personality. The following unique document appeared, written in a kind of shorthand:

QUESTION: Why?
ANSWER: Don't know, afraid to know.
Q: Who?
A: D [Damon].
Q: Who does?
A: Me.
Q: Me?
A: Me—Brown—B.
Q: Explain.
A: D is D; B is B.
Q: B know D?
A: Yes.
Q: D know B? [Does Damon know Brown?]
A: No. No.
Q: B part of D?
A: No. B is B; D is D.
Q: Can I talk to B?
A: Are! [You are doing it!]
Q: Talk to D?
A: Want to. [If you want to.]
Q: How long have you been B?
A: Always.
Q: What do you want?
A: Help D.

Q: Why?
A: D afraid.
Q: Do you know what D is afraid of?
A: Yes; D no. ["No" stands for "know."]
Q: Why?
A: D afraid, forgot, don't want to know.
Q: Think D should?
A: Yes, yes, yes.
Q: You know what it is?
A: Yes.
Q: Why don't you tell D?
A: Can't, can't.
Q: Why?
A: D afraid, afraid.
Q: And you?
A: Afraid a little, not so much.

The other personality, "Miss Brown," was entirely a separate entity and able to enter into a spirited dialogue with the investigator as well as with Miss Damon. A section of the report read:

> She would interrupt an attempted explanation by Miss Damon by writing "Wrong," and would respond to stimuli and cues which Miss Damon either overlooked completely or misunderstood. In fact she so impressed her personality upon those in the office that automatically she was regarded by the entire group as a distinct personality among them. Nor was Brown limited just to the problems at hand. She would enter readily into conversations on many other topics, often resorting to this in an effort to distract the investigator from his efforts. In addition Brown was possessed of a definite sense of personal pride; on two occasions she resented derogatory re-

marks Damon made about her, and thereupon refused to write anything more except "won't" until Damon apologized.

Miss Brown was very impatient with the investigators' inability to understand her shorthand ("Yo"—meaning "I don't know," etc.). Erickson found that Miss Brown was highly protective to Miss Damon, "shielding her, demanding special consideration for her, offering encouragement, distracting her attention, deliberately deceiving her and employing various other protective devices." Typical of this attitude is the following piece of automatic writing representing Miss Brown's views:

Writing means a lot, B know it all. D don't, can't, afraid, forgot something a long time ago. D can't remember because she never knew some of it, she just thought she did but she didn't. B afraid to tell D, D get awful scared, afraid, cry. B don't like D scared, won't let her be scared, won't let her feel bad. B need help. Erickson ask. Ask right question, B tell Erickson right answer; wrong question, wrong answer. Right question only right question. B just answer, not tell, won't tell because D afraid, awful afraid, Erickson ask, ask, ask. Brown answer, not tell, question answer, not tell, question, answer, that help. B answer but not too fast because D get scared, cry, sick. B tell truth, all truth, Erickson not understand because he don't know. B trying to tell, Erickson don't ask right questions. Ask, ask, ask. B can't tell, won't tell. B a little afraid; B only answer. Ask, ask.

Eventually, recalled events in Miss Damon's childhood rationalize her obsessions, but neither investigator was able to explain the presence of Miss Brown. Eventually

206

they decided that the possessing spirit was a good one and was a highly developed alter ego. Erickson and Kubie concluded their report by stating:

> The story makes it evident that under the impulse of terror and anger, the young woman had made a very deep and painful identification of herself with her grandfather. Somehow all her later anxieties and compulsions stemmed from this momentous event. At some time she built up a protective, compassionate alter ego, Jane Brown, who knew the things that she did not want to know, who was either unable or else forbidden to tell them to anyone but who exercised an almost continuously protective role toward the patient herself.

There is no record as to whether exorcism was involved to "clear" the alter ego, but it would seem unlikely. Therefore the pronounced and protective alter ego personality stayed permanently with Miss Damon. But its principal use was now over—and Miss Damon never had reason to recall Miss Brown.

Records in Washington for January 1949 concern the possession of a fourteen-year-old boy. The first indications were loud, scratching sounds that appeared to come from both walls and attic. A rodent extermination company failed to find any rats or mice whatsoever, although the sounds continued to increase during their investigations, particularly when the boy, Douglas Deen, was in proximity. Then, poltergeist activity became apparent, with flying dishes and furniture moving back and forth of their own volition. Footsteps sounded continuously across the hall. The bed in which Douglas slept also began to tremble.

Finally, the distraught family called in the Reverend Winston, pastor of their church in the Washington suburb of Mount Rainier. The pastor asked the boy into his home and then related to a closed meeting (on August 9, 1949) of the Society for Parapsychology exactly what had happened there. Sleeping beside the boy in a twin bed, the Reverend Winston did not have long to wait for activity. After about ten minutes the bed in which the boy was sleeping began to vibrate violently. Scraping and scratching noises also came from the walls. The minister then scrutinized the boy carefully, reassuring himself that there was no way the boy could be responsible for what was happening. He then placed the boy in a huge and very heavy armchair. Shortly afterward the armchair rose three inches and moved in the direction of the wall until it could go no further. At this point the chair tilted and threw the boy onto the floor.

The Reverend Winston then placed the boy on a pallet. This slid across the floor and under one of the beds. In both instances the boy's hands remained outside the bedding, his body was rigid, and the blankets showed no signs of wrinkling. After unsuccessful medical and psychiatric treatment at Georgetown Hospital and at St. Louis University Hospital, Douglas was handed over to the Jesuits. Exorcism took two and a half months, during which the Jesuit priest concerned lived on bread, water and prayer—the purpose of the fast being to fortify him against the powers of Satan. Finally he ordered the evil spirit to leave Douglas's body with the following prayer:

> I command you, whoever you are, unclean spirit, and all of your associates obsessing this friend of God, that by the mysteries of the Incarnation, Passion, Resurrection, and Ascension of Our Lord Jesus Christ, by the mission, the Holy Spirit, and by the coming of the same Master, for the Judgement, give

me your name, the day and the hour of your exit, together with some sign, and even though I am an unworthy minister of God, I command thee to obey in all these things nor ever again in any manner to offend this creature of God, or those who are here or any of their possessions.

The reaction from the boy was traditional. He flew into violent anger and began to tremble violently. In a high and shrill voice he spoke very rapidly in Latin (a language of which he knew not one word) or broke into abuse, blasphemy and cursing of the obscene kind. The ritual was repeated many times until, in May 1949, Douglas fell silent and uttered no more imprecations. His body remained passive, as did the furniture. From that moment on the boy returned completely to normal and no further signs of possession were reported.

I have already established the Church's attitude to exorcism, although it must be made clear that some of the evangelical churches and some aspects of the charismatic movement are obsessed with unclean spirits and are often to be seen publicly removing them in their services— amid great scenes of hysteria. But there are double motives here, and in many cases exorcism is used as a means of binding a frightened, bewildered and rootless flock even closer to the movement. The case of the Midlands exorcism which ended in fatality is the most obvious type of casualty resulting from such activity. But however suspect the exorcism is, and however doubtful the motives behind the ritual are, it is clearly a very dangerous practice. Before I discuss the work of some of the leading exorcists, here are two more recent cases of exorcism, both of which were very well documented and witnessed by a large number of people.

In San Francisco in 1973 a family claimed to have suf-

fered a good deal of supernatural phenomena. This began
with poltergeist activity and continued with the appearance of mysterious black shadows, the outbreak of small
fires, the vanishing of various objects, later their broken
reappearance, and the attempted strangling by demons of
the couple concerned. After priests, psychologists and
mediums had failed to halt all these alarming events, a
Jesuit priest named the Reverend Karl Patzelt was con-
sulted. Eventually he sought permission from his arch-
bishop to perform the Roman ritual and this permission
was given.

Equipped with fragments of the holy cross itself, Patzelt conducted the exorcism thirteen times before it was
successful. He also conducted the ritual amid a storm of
criticism. The Reverend Richard Byfield said that "using
the full rite was like using a twenty-inch gun to kill mos-
quitoes. To think that the Prince of Darkness himself—a
one-time archangel—would stoop to petty arson and leg-
erdemain with kitchen knives is trying on the imagination. After all, Satan has such a vaunting pride he defied
God." Another indignant critic was the Reverend Peter
Riga of St. Mary's College in San Francisco. He deplored
the apparent belief "in the medieval superstition of
possession, obsession and Devil wizardry." But Patzelt
replied to his critics by firmly stating: "There is value in
all of this as it brings out the reality of the Devil. If the
Devil is real then God must be."

A year later, in the North of England, a sixteen-year-old
girl claimed to be possessed by a dead pop star. As in the
case of Douglas Deen the possession began after she had
been using a Ouija board. The spirit apparently made a
continuous stream of sexual suggestions to her, and her
orgiastic fantasies were so frantic that it took two or
three people to hold her down. The girl also shrieked out
the obscenities that have come to be associated with

210

possession and began to believe that the pop star wished her dead "so that they could be together." When the local vicar arrived he found the girl unconscious on the floor and one of her friends, another girl, singing in "a deep American male voice." An exorcism was carried out but this proved to be ineffective. After a period in a psychiatric hospital, the girl's condition improved. On her return home the possession reoccurred but a second exorcism, involving the entire house, cleared the situation up completely. The girl is now entirely normal.

The New Catholic Encyclopedia states, "Psychiatry has shown that the working of the subconscious may explain many, if not most, of the abnormal activities that earlier generations had attributed to diabolical activity." Certainly our knowledge of psychiatry, parapsychiatry, telekinesis, telepathy, and extrasensory perception continues to increase. But of possession there is little knowledge, and explanations concerning hysteria and obsession are barely satisfactory in face of the mass of evidence for the inexplicable.

There is no question of a real, living demon entering anybody's mind. But there *is* a question of guilt, sexual longing, religious fervor and fear stirring the mind into accepting that it is possessed by an evil spirit. Throughout this book one theme has repeatedly emerged—that of hell not being a literal pit but a mental creation by the evil parts of ourselves. Possession falls into exactly the same category.

But what of the exorcists themselves? How balanced and objective are they? The majority of modern exorcists are extremely suspect, and even those commissioned by the Church of England are far from reliable. Subjectivity and hysteria intrude all too often, and it is only the rare individual who is able to bring objectivity and nonhysterical spirituality to the situation. There are four men worth noting as exorcists—Catholic Father Theophilus Riesinger, whom I have already discussed in connection with the Iowa case; and Christopher Neil-Smith and John Pearce-Higgins, Protestant priests who are still at work as exorcists today. I have already described the work of Dr. Martin Israel, who, in my opinion, is by far the most convincing of all. It must be said, however, that all these four men believe in demons as entities and not as the symbolized evil of the mind.

Up to 1936, Riesinger claimed to have exorcised twenty-two people after the Iowa case had made him so controversially famous. A newspaper account commented on the pamphlet written on the Iowa case by the Reverend Celestine Kapsner of St. Johns Abbey, Collegeville, Minnesota. The pamphlet had the official imprimatur of the Bishop of St. Cloud. The newspaper stated:

> While no Catholic is required to believe in any particular account of a case of diabolical possession outside those set forth in the Scriptures, nevertheless, numbers of people, through the centuries, have testified to the actuality of demoniac possession and to the efficacy of exorcism as it is conducted according to the dogma of the Catholic Church.
>
> Saint Mark tells of the seven devils that Christ cast out of Mary Magdalen; Saint Luke, of the legion of devils that, at divine command, went out of the wretched creature who lived in the tombs, and entered into a herd of swine which ran down a hill and into a lake.

Riesinger had a number of yardsticks by which he could define "real" possession as opposed to "imagined." He was convinced that the possessed were able to communicate with dogs and cats. Unfortunately, Riesinger was given to making the most enigmatic of statements at times—statements that would often cloud his credibility. For instance, asked why the possessed chose to have dialogues with cats and dogs, he replied, "I do not know, except that as a rule we call the Devil a dog. We call him a hellish dog. Once when I called a devil I was exorcising a diabolical dog, he made the rejoinder that he did not care for that 'I am a dog, anyway,' he said."

Riesinger went on to comment:

> I admit that . . . symptoms look like hysteria and insanity, but that is not the case. Through exorcism and through the prayers of the Church we can force the devils to talk. . . . I would always prefer to work in secret, but sometimes the devils make such a howl that I cannot keep it quiet.

Certainly Satan was more than vocal with Riesinger and could be quite testy at times. For instance, during the course of one exorcism, Riesinger mispronounced a word. Angrily Satan replied, "Dumbbell, you don't know anything."

But despite Riesinger's alarming anecdotes, there is no doubt that he was a serious exorcist. He was aware not only of the danger in which he was living but also the danger that his assistants faced. He claimed that Satan tried to take revenge countless times, including sending a plague of "hell rats" against him and his assistants. He also claimed that so strong and vindictive was this revenge that priests rarely lived for more than two years after their first exorcism. Luckily, Riesinger was excused this fate for he was sure that "God has given me an extra gift of strength."

The same gift of strength must have been given to Christopher Neil-Smith, who performed his first exorcism in 1949 and now exorcises at the rate of about 500 a year. Typical examples of his methods are contained in the following account. Neil-Smith writes:

One of the most frightening experiences I have had was when the Chaplain of a prison asked me to come and exorcise two Hell's Angels in the Prison Chapel. Here there was clearly no doubt about the violence, one had been sentenced for malicious wounding with a knife and the other with holding a gun with intent to harm. The strangest thing about it was why they asked to be exorcised. They explained that they had been connected with black magic and had dedicated themselves to the devil to harm others. They had now become afraid that when they left the prison they might murder someone and would not be able to control themselves. They were almost afraid to go into the Chapel because of their former connection with black magic. The first man went out into unconsciousness under the exorcism and was brought round with holy water. The second man went dazed and later came round. Eventually when they had recovered their equilibrium they said they had lost all fear of the Chapel and asked for a bible. A Franciscan brother who had attended them produced a bible and we read Mark 5 about the violent men. They then said it spoke to their condition and asked questions about the Church. They had clearly been "possessed."

Another case of Hell's Angels was that of a young man in Borstal, imprisoned for participating in gang violence. In this case I was asked to exorcise him with the psychiatrist and the probation officer present. Both the psychiatrist and the probation officer said that they were shattered by the experience and

214

recognised the tremendous power of the evil force that possessed him but never for one moment questioned the need for exorcism. The young man was cleared.

Another case was one of a young man who was permitted by a Roman Catholic psychiatrist to be brought out of a mental hospital accompanied by a male nurse for exorcism. He had tried to strangle his mother with a strange violence but it subsided after the exorcism and he was later able to be rehabilitated. Both these men showed similar symptoms of violence to the demoniacs in the Gospels and reveal the relevance of possession as mentioned in the Gospels to our modern life today.

Neil-Smith has been brought in with cases of arson, witchcraft, satanism, voodoo, cursing, black magic, Ouija boards, ghosts, drugs, hypnosis and other conditions too numerous to mention. His exorcisms are completely interdenominational and he has been accepted as an exorcist by faiths ranging from the Roman Catholic to the Russian and Greek Orthodox, and from the Lutherans to the Methodists, Baptists and Congregationalists. Neil-Smith agrees with Dr. Israel when it comes to serious diabolical exorcism. He points out:

The Devil is always intent on destroying priests. The Roman Ritual is wise in asserting that the qualities required in an exorcist are "prudence, piety and moral integrity." If a priest is going to act as an exorcist in a specialist ministry he must recognise the dangers—the chinks in his armour which are hate, fear, doubt and illicit sex—otherwise he may play into the hands of the devil and the forces he is trying to destroy may end up destroying him.

Neil-Smith regards the ability to exorcise as a gift. He also sees love and hate as similar to good and evil. This can be seen as a reminder of the duality of the forces of good and evil discussed earlier in this book. The preacher Harry Williams best summarizes this simplistically:

We all have experience of two types of feeling. There is the feeling which unites us to our world and makes us rejoice in it, an experience of love, of acceptance, of communion. And there is the other kind of feeling which separates us from our world and makes us hate it, an experience of fear, of exile, of discord. The first of these feelings belongs more truly to us than the second. We are profoundly satisfied by love and communion. We are exasperated by exile and hatred. . . . The difference between these two types of feeling is the difference between good and evil and evil is secondary, existing not in its own right but as thwarted goodness.

John Pearce-Higgins' most interesting case of possession concerned a "Mrs. Martin" who had written to him about a "presence" which had originally been passive and who had now grown troublesome. Her letter described the symptoms as follows:

The "ghost" was already here when we took up our residence thirty years ago, but apart from moving things about and occasionally kicking the foot of the bed, it caused no inconvenience in our lives, so we did not trouble about it. However, in the last six years it has become a nuisance. It persistently disturbs my sleep. I awake to sense it bending over me, breathing very heavily, like someone dying, and it will repeat this as many as six or eight times in one night. Strangely enough it does not disturb my husband, but he too has heard this breathing when he is up and about. It also walks about the bedroom at night, and again the tread is a very heavy one, making the floor vibrate under its weight.

Quite recently I awoke one morning at eight o'clock to find it snoring loudly beside me—my husband was in the kitchen making the early morning tea—and what is more, I could still hear this snoring whilst I got out of bed and put on my dressing gown. Mrs. [Alexandra], who lives only a few doors away, can *see* this "ghost," and a couple of weeks ago she very kindly performed an "exorcism" but it was of no avail. We had only four good nights' rest before it was back again and up to its old tricks. She then came in with a view to ascertaining the reason for its speedy return, only to be told that he did not like his wife—he apparently also assumes that this house belongs to him and that we are intruders.

If you could help in this matter it would be very much appreciated, as it is beginning to get on top of us. Should you require further information, Mrs. [Alexandra] has very kindly offered her services as we are not on the telephone.

Although this was not strictly a case of possession, Pearce-Higgins decided to treat it as important for it had implications of a far worse situation to come. Although not psychic himself, the Reverend Canon John D. Pearce-Higgins is chairman of the Committee on the Study of Psychic Phenomena for the Churches' Fellowship for Psychical and Spiritual Studies in the United Kingdom. He works with two healers and during 1971 and 1972 the team were approached for spiritual help in some 3,000 cases. Of these, 540 appealed for "psychic help" in defense against possessions or haunting. In 180 of these hauntings the team defined 40 as genuinely psychic. Of the remaining 500, 113 were regarded as genuine cases of possession, while the others were defined as either emotional disturbances or hallucinatory or delusionary. By 1974 Pearce-Higgins was stating that "an increasing incidence of mental disturbances employ the language and symbolism of an obviously spurious brand of spiritualism." He believes that success is due to teamwork and that

> in contact healing we work with a minimum of ritual or dressing up, particularly in cases of personal possession as the power which flows through my healer friends' hands seems sufficient to extrude the possessing entity. Sometimes this produces various stretchings or contortions of the patient's body, but no words are spoken until the end, which I modify the prayer of "exorcism" into a thanksgiving that God has removed the entity. This fact becomes apparent from the changes in the possessed person's appearance and manner—a cure in fact.

To take an example, one possessed man wriggled and stretched during the process of healing and then fell into a mildly catatonic state in which he slid off his chair and finished up actually kneeling on the floor. In another case the team visited a young woman who was apparently inhabited by the spirit of a young man "who had been stabbed to death during an altercation outside the woman's house and who had somehow managed to possess her for a short time." As the spirit of the young man was exorcised, Pearce-Higgins claims that the process of extrusion seemed to move upward from the lower part of the young woman's body. Then the woman's neck swelled up as if she had some gigantic growth and only returned to normal as the spirit passed out of her body.

"After a good night's sleep," reported Pearce-Higgins, "she telephoned me in the morning and said she felt fine."

But in the case of Mrs. Martin the situation was infinitely more subtle. On investigation Mrs. Martin turned out to be a sprightly fifty-eight-year-old who was very deaf. Her husband was an old-age pensioner. Pearce-Higgins then put her to a test which he explained in the following terms:

We find that if the patient, when treated by laying on of hands on the head or near the face, begins to display very rapid flickering movements of the eyelids and eyelashes, this indicates a psychological problem stemming from the subconscious mind, and is not a case of possession by an external entity. Mrs. Martin showed only a very slight degree of flickering, not uncommon, as many people have slight but not seriously schizophrenic tendencies. This did not seem commensurate with the degree of phenomena reported. In view of the strength of the evidence indicated by the medium's report, we were in some doubt and decided that this was a case that merited a visit to the house. As it turned out we should have had more confidence in our own criteria.

Indeed they should, for what Pearce-Higgins was about to witness was a very strong case of autosuggestion. The reason for detailing it below is because many cases of haunting or possession are clearly caused by autosuggestion, and they are not necessarily any the *less* fearsome for the sufferer as a result. Also there is obviously still every reason for exorcism in such cases.

Owing to the fact that his two healers were wanted elsewhere, Canon Pearce-Higgins visited the Martin household on his own. There he found the atmosphere normal and with no indication of a presence. (In Pearce-Higgins' view the rooms should have had a thick, soupy, heavy atmosphere, with patches of unnatural cold.) Nevertheless he held a short service and both the Martins took holy communion. There were a number of books on spiritualism and yoga in the house and when Pearce-Higgins asked Mr. Martin if he could hear the heavy snoring he replied that he had eliminated it from his consciousness by mental control. This, allied with Mrs. Martin's extreme deafness, made Pearce-Higgins wonder about the "objectivity of the phenomena." Some days later he received a letter from the Martins pointing out that the presence was still there and that his efforts had been as unsuccessful as Mrs. Alexandra's. Pearce-Higgins was puzzled because in all other cases the requiem mass that he had performed in the Martins' household had always been successful in the past. Nevertheless, he decided to pursue the case and made a second visit to the Martins. This time he ensured that both the healers and Mrs. Alexandra were present.

The team first went to Mrs. Alexandra's house where they heard enough garbled explanations to disquieten them considerably. They then saw Mrs. Martin, who gave them the new information that six years earlier her much loved sister had died of cancer. As she died she had been through serious contortions and her breathing had been highly stentorian. In other words she had shown all the usual effects of terminal illness, effects that her sister, Mrs. Martin, had never witnessed before. Directly after the death of her sister, Mrs. Martin had come under the influence of the doubtful powers of Mrs. Alexandra, and on several occasions had received vague communications that were meant to have come from her sister. It was then that the "snoring" phenomenon became apparent. Then her husband admitted to the team that he had, in fact, never heard the snoring and had only told his wife that he had because he was afraid that she was losing her sanity.

The entire situation was now clearly subjective and entirely based on the autosuggestion of the dying sister and the suspect medium. Gently, Pearce-Higgins pointed this out to Mrs. Martin, hoping that her basic intelligence would eventually accept it. After a relapse during which she heard the snoring again, Mrs. Martin gradually came to accept that what had been happening had been created by her own mind and not by an outside force. Later she came along to Pearce-Higgins' clinic where

She somewhat disturbed me by saying that she had an inquiring mind and since our second visit to the house she had been reading furiously to try to find out what had caused the trouble. This seemed to indicate that she was still subconsciously working on the "spirit" hypothesis and reluctant to relinquish it. I was firm in telling her that she must absolutely put out of her mind any idea that these voices had any "spirit" origin, that she should stop reading spiritualist-type literature for at least six months or until she was completely free from hearing the voices; otherwise she might find herself in trouble again.

Finally Mrs. Martin completely recovered and on a subsequent visit made by Pearce-Higgins she revealed more of the motivation behind the claims that she had made. She told him that she and her sister had been virtually deserted by their parents and they had been brought up together in a convent. They had always been very close and were completely devoted to each other. She had been a student of spiritual knowledge and had followed what she termed "the path" to "God's power." When Mrs. Martin realized that her sister was dying she became determined to hold on to her and, through spiritual-

221

ism, bring her back. She claimed to have realized that Mrs. Alexandra was issuing meaningless statements and messages. She said that she had thanked God for the intervention of Pearce-Higgins and his team and had accepted that what had happened was all in her mind. She also realized that she had been quite wrong to "hang on" to her sister in such a manner. All the phenomena, she concluded, had now ceased.

This case shows not only the vast subjectivity involved in possession, but also how a human being can desperately clutch on to a departed spirit and almost bring it unwillingly to life again. The spirit of Mrs. Martin's dead sister emerged in Mrs. Martin's own mind, but had it not been for the sensible intervention of Pearce-Higgins and his healing team there is every possibility that complete "possession" would have occurred and that this could well have quickly become uncontrolled.

When a "real" exorcism is required, Pearce-Higgins and his two healers conduct a short service of holy communion, and a requiem mass for the release of the earthbound spirit. Then he goes through the house with a bowl of holy or blessed water and makes the sign of a Celtic cross in the name of the Holy Trinity on each wall, door, window and mirror in the rooms where the possession has taken place.

Canon Pearce-Higgins is also well aware of the dualism problem. But he counters this with the doctrine of fallen angels. Demons, he considers, are fallen angels and they remain children of God. He also believes, because of this, that demons are ultimately redeemable.

He goes on to say that he has no wish to send any demon, however powerful, into eternal damnation. In fact he finds it difficult to believe that the limited powers of man *can* condemn anyone or anything to eternal damnation. But just in case this drastic exile could be commanded he has altered the words in his exorcism to read:

"In the authority of Christ, I command you to be taken hence and bound fast as with chains and cast into darkness, from which there is no return save through repentance," or "until the day of repentance, so that you trouble no more the servants of God." He regards this as the equivalent of a prison sentence.

Canon Pearce-Higgins finds the commission on exorcism too rigid in its definitions. For instance it states:

> Christian exorcism is the binding of evil powers by the triumph of Christ Jesus, through the application of the power demonstrated by that triumph, in and by his Church. The New Testament not only assumes the existence of non-human powers of evil, it asserts repeatedly the fact of the triumph of Christ Jesus over them. The prominence given in the gospels to the exorcisms done by our Lord is evidence of this, as is also the close association with them in the word *exousia*.
>
> It will be as well at the outset to note that in Christian usage the verb to *exorcise* applies strictly only to demons. It is possible to speak loosely about exorcising persons or places, but what is meant is the exorcising of the demonic forces of evil *in* those persons or places. Exorcism is an exercise of *exousia*: it commands and binds.

Pearce-Higgins feels, however:

> It would be foolish for me or anyone categorically to state the "demons" or "evil forces" do not exist. We have seen far too much terrible evil and cruelty in our time not to recognize the existence of a demonic element in human nature and sometimes in its environment. These forces appear to be purposively malevolent and destructive; in other words,

223

they appear to be using reason for bad ends. The thought behind them is evil. That this thought can clothe itself in the traditional visual, auditory or sensory imagery of "the devil"—with horns, hooves, tails and smells—and terrifying sensory hallucinations is regrettably probable. But in the normal cases which we find in haunted houses and in cases of mental and behavioral disturbance due to possession by low grade, discarnate spirits, the exorcising of "demons" as a formula, in my experience simply does not work.

Finally, Canon Pearce-Higgins is very concerned that exorcism should be progressive and not steeped in paranoia.

God forbid that we should return to the mentality of the times of the "Devils of Loudun," which—a priori—saw diabolism or witchcraft in every shadow, in every unusual physical or mental state. But surely the massive achievements of the scientific method are a sufficient protection against this. Here we are dealing with the frontier area between the normal and the paranormal, the psychological and the parapsychological, whose existence science is loath to admit, while yet being unable to account for or deal with it.

Inevitably, the problem about exorcism has been its victims and its counsellors. Satanism, as we have already seen, was created and made dangerous by its practitioners. The same applies to exorcism. No amount of reports, investigations, rulings and sanctions will ever remove the real dangers—the subjectivity, the *need* to be possessed—and the vicariousness of dabbling with the supernatural. Loneliness, the desperate need for a faith and

224

lack of either sexual or personal fulfillment make many people anxious to be possessed—and equally anxious to produce the symptoms the exorcist wants to see and hear. As far as the exorcist is concerned, there are similar reasons for frailty. In this chapter I have tried to describe the genuine type of exorcist, but obviously there are thousands more who are not. Nevertheless, despite all this human weakness and subjectivity, the big question remains. Are there really forces of evil waiting to possess the human mind and body? Dr. Martin Israel believes there are: "Demonic possession is rare but it can happen. And when it does it is of enormous strength." But even these dark forces, he believes, should be treated with love and reconciliation, and here he is as one with the other leading exorcists. It is significant that the true exorcist preaches love and reconciliation while the false exorcist preaches only of sin and damnation—the very foundations of hell itself. Indeed, the exorcist is more often the instrument of the Devil rather than the instrument of God.

An extreme example of demonic exorcists can be seen in the 1969 trial in Switzerland of John Stocker and Magdalena Kohler. They stood accused of murdering a teenage girl named Bernadette Hasler. The murder took place in a small village outside Zurich in 1966. Stocker and Kohler began a religious cult as a result of meeting a Carmelite nun known as Sister Stella. They met her on a so-called pilgrimage to Jerusalem and found that she claimed to have a "direct telephone line to heaven." This arrangement was made even more convenient by the fact that she set down her "heavenly messages" on a typewriter. Sister Stella became a "child" to Stocker and Kohler, and Magdalena Kohler confirmed this by stating, "Herr Stocker was the father, I was the mother, and Stella was the child." Magdalena gave Stella a red teddy bear because she was "ordered by God."

Magdalena Kohler was possibly the more fanatical of the two, and she believed that the end of the world was soon to emerge in true apocalyptic style. In Germany the cult had a building in which one room was reserved for the pope—a sanctuary that he was to seek directly the day of catastrophe arrived. Naturally the Holy Family, as the Stocker/Kohler relationship termed itself, would be "saved" from that devastating day of judgment—as would their adherents. During the course of their union with Sister Stella, the nun was twice ordered to return to the convent by her superiors and twice abducted by Stocker and Kohler. Sister Stella afterward wrote:

> Times were not as good as here in the Cloister. I no longer had a will of my own, and I was in constant inner fear. I was spoken to as if I were a child. Today I no longer play with dolls. I no longer write Messages from the Saviour. I was suffering from a malignant delusion.

Sister Stella's messages, however, were extremely convenient for Stocker and Kohler. She prophesied, for instance, that the world would end with a hail of brimstone. Magdalena actually gave birth to a child, but I can find no record of exactly what happened to it. Certainly both Stocker and Kohler had a fixation about child substitutes and their need to dominate them. But the next child-substitution ended in tragedy. The situation began when Stocker and Kohler were forced to leave Germany and settle in Switzerland on the farm of the Haslers, who were quick to join the cult which was now called The International Family Society for the Advancement of Peace. The farm, well stocked against the day on which the world was to end, was known locally as Noah's Ark. Almost immediately the Haslers' daughter, Bernadette, came under the influence of Stocker and Kohler. They told the teenage girl that they were now her "holy parents," that they would give her "divine education" and that she was no longer permitted to speak to her own parents. Meanwhile, the parents had their mail censored, their money and food administered and their car taken over for "missionary trips." Later Josef Hasler was forbidden to speak to his wife at all and not allowed to visit her in hospital where she was giving birth to a premature baby. At the trial Hasler was to say of Stocker and Kohler, "If I had to judge those two today, I would beat them to a pulp and feed them to the pigs."

Meanwhile the cult grew, particularly when Bernadette announced that she had made a pact with the Devil. Confessions were wrung out of her, although it was clear that these confessions were largely the work of her "holy parents." The confessions made such statements as, "I have taken communion improperly 6,000 times; I have prayed wrongly 450 times; I have given 750 tongue kisses; 1,000 times have I undertaken the sexual act in my imagination." She was also purported to have written, "I love the Devil. He is beautiful. He visits me nearly every night. He is much better than God. I would like to belong only to the Devil."

Sadism began when the cult attempted to drive out the unclean spirits from Bernadette's soul. She was turned into a domestic slave, forbidden to go for walks, had her violin lessons stopped and was not allowed to mix with the other unfortunate children who had entered the cult and were being dominated by the "holy parents." Magdalena Kohler heaped imprecations on Bernadette, calling her a "lying swine" and a "perverted piece" as well as "Satan's mate" and the "Devil's whore." Magdalena Kohler also induced confessions involving a marriage to Satan which the wretched Bernadette described as follows: "I wore a white dress and he had his black, shiny feet. It was a beautiful picture."

Exorcism, Stocker and Kohler style, involved two beatings a day, administered by the "holy parents" as well as other members of the cult. Then, on May 14, 1966, frenzy overtook the cult and Bernadette was forced to crouch on the bed with her backside exposed. She was then beaten with whips, canes and a plastic pipe. She was also forced to eat her own excretia. Next morning she was dead owing to an embolism of the lungs. Her body was a mass of bruises and abrasions.

The reason behind Bernadette's pact with the Devil became clear later—she had been denied Easter confession by Magdalena Kohler and as a result she sought out the Devil as a better God than Magdalena's crazy deity. At the trial Magdalena Kohler said:

> I have, in everything I did, acted under orders from God. All force, and all that has happened, was done on divine instruction. To avoid discipline, or faith, to withhold oneself from divine orders, leads the soul to punishment in hell and eternal damnation.

Seizing this statement, her defense tried to prove that Magdalena Kohler was

> . . . a simple-minded woman who grew up in an environment of narrow superstition and fear of eternal damnation. She is convinced that, one day, she will have to fight a duel with the Devil.

But on February 4, 1969, the court at Zurich sentenced Stocker and Kohler to ten years in prison while their minions received shorter sentences. The state attorney, John Lohner, stated that the sentences were "a warning to all those still enmeshed in superstitions and in abusing religious faith." He went on to urge the Roman Catholic authorities to help in "cleansing the soil that nurtures belief in and fear of the Devil, so that such crimes as that against Bernadette Hasler may never be repeated." The vicar general of the Canton of Zurich, Monseigneur Alfred Teobaldi, pointed out that the cult had originated in Germany and told the public to be on their guard against "the influence of movements originating in foreign countries." He also stated, in defense of the Catholic Church, that "no Church can be protected against members who use holy works as a pretext to practise diabolic actions." But were Stocker and Kohler acting under diabolical influence? Or were they mentally ill? The theological expert at the Zurich court, Dr. Nigg, agreed that the following two arguments held weight. Firstly that "the influence of evil forces in the world cannot be denied." Secondly that "if the influence of demonic power is categorically denied, world history becomes incomprehensible. Life consists of a struggle between good and evil forces. It does not matter what names we give to these powers." Nigg went on to say that there was a possibility that Stocker and Kohler were under the influence of the demonic. He said that "the perpetrators were surrounded by demons who had succeeded in confusing their minds so totally that they forgot even the most basic elements of humanity."

Finally, another case where two exorcists are on trial as this book goes to press. Two Roman Catholic priests, Ernst Alt and Wilhelm Renz, are on trial in Aschaffenburg, in Northern Bavaria, accused of the manslaughter of a girl who died after exorcism rites. At twenty-three, Anneliese Michel wasted away to about sixty pounds while the two exorcists were trying to exorcise the devils which they believed possessed her. She died in July 1976 after eleven months of Church-approved rituals. The British *Daily Telegraph* reported on March 30, 1978:

Father Wilhelm Renz, 67, a member of the Salvatorian order, Father Ernst Alt, 40, a parish priest, Joseph Michel, 61 and his wife, Anna, 57, were accused of homicide through negligence by failing to summon medical aid.

All pleaded not guilty.

Immediately the trial opened, the defense challenged the indictment, saying that West Germany's constitution guarantees freedom of belief and religion and that Fräulein Michel had refused medical help because of her "strong will based on religious beliefs."

Later her father asked everyone in court to join him in a short prayer, but the judge replied, "If you want to pray, you can do it alone."

The defense called for the return of tape recordings in which it is alleged the priests described how they cast out six demons. These included the wide range of Judas, Nero and Hitler (identified by his shouts of "Sieg Heil"). The indictment alleged that Fräulein Michel died of "highly advanced emaciation" in her parents' home in the village of Klingenberg, after refusing food and water. The indictment went on to say that her death "could have been prevented with all likelihood" if medical help had been provided.

Fräulein Michel had received medical treatment for epilepsy between 1969 and 1975 but had become convinced that she was possessed by demons when treatment failed. This was alleged by the prosecution when the charges were first made. Apparently Bishop Josef Stangl approved the exorcism on the recommendation of a Jesuit priest, Father Adolf Rodewyk, who was an expert on the rite as described in the *Rituale Romanum* of 1614 (see beginning of chapter) and appointed Fathers Renz and Alt to carry out the ritual. The prosecutor, Karl Stenger, also pointed out that the bishop's role had been investigated but he was not indicted. Stenger stated:

"Bishop Stangl assumed that medical help was being used. The opposite could not be proved."

After Fräulein Michel's death, relations insisted on her exhumation after a nun had had a vision of the body miraculously preserved, marred only by the stigmata on hands and feet. Father Renz and the girl's parents were at the graveside for the exhumation. However, the authorities who inspected the body said that it showed merely the decay normal after two years.

Perhaps the real answer to possession lies in this case history produced by Professor Hans Holzer.

Mary Y. is engaged to be married to a young man of her acquaintance. After a few short weeks the young man is killed in a street accident. Shortly after the funeral, Mary receives spirit communication from the deceased. Thus far, the relationship is entirely within the realm of possibility, as seen by the open-minded psychical researcher. After a while, Mary becomes convinced that she cannot ever forget her dead fiancé nor find another to take his place. To the psychologist this is a simple matter. Mary's mind is becoming unhinged due to excessive grief and her inability to adjust to the environment. But from the parapsychological point of view, something else may be happening. When an occasional communication from the deceased, generally through the mediumship of some local clairvoyant or similar person, is no longer sufficient for Mary, and her entire life becomes oriented toward a resumption of the relationship with her dead fiancé, she reaches out to him in the hope of reestablishing a link. At this moment obsession takes place. In Mary's case this obsession may lead to suicide in the hope of joining her loved one on the other side of life. That this is a fallacy can be seen in the light of evidence that suicides rarely reach their goal on the other side of life, but are, to the contrary, sent "back to school," as it were, to make up that which they tried to escape on earth.

Since Mary does not commit suicide and since she cannot be on the same level as her fiance, she becomes obsessed with him and their further love tie. The continuing relationship develops between two equal partners, one of the flesh and one in the spirit. As a result of this, Mary shuns all physical relationships on the earth plane, devoting herself entirely to her spirit lover.

In this instance Mary created her own possession. She is not unique. Throughout a lonely world there are many isolated people who, for a variety of reasons, *need* to be possessed. Although the subjects of many of the case histories and the view of many of the exorcists in this chapter have claimed that demons exist as separate invading entities, I find this hard to accept. Surely it is the contortions of the mind that are producing the demons, not the demons who are entering the mind. This does not mean that the situation is any the less dangerous; nor does it mean that the rites of exorcism are any the less vital. It simply brings me to the conclusion that possession is self-created but nevertheless just as demonic as the presence of an outside force. Possession is a separate condition well removed from physical or mental illness, although both may play some small part in its makeup. If my argument is to be accepted and possession is seen as a separate and specific state of mind, then it is worth investigating in a separate and specific way. Everyone accepts that many of the secrets of the mind are as yet unrevealed to us. Surely this mystical and terrifying secret is a classic example.

PART EIGHT

The Devil in Art and Literature

As we have seen in earlier chapters, the Devil appears in many different forms in both art and literature. Milton sees Satan as the fallen leader in *Paradise Lost*:

> The warlike Angel moved,
> Disdainfully half smiling, thus replied:
> "O loss of one in Heaven to judge of wise,
> Since Satan fell, whom folly overthrew,
> And now returns him from his prison scaped,
> Gravely in doubt whether to hold them wise
> Or not who ask what boldness brought him hither
> Unlicensed from his bounds in Hell prescribed!
> So wise he judges it to fly from pain
> However, and to scape his punishment!
> So judge thou still, presumptuous, till the wrath,
> Which thou incurr'st by flying, meet thy flight
> Sevenfold, and scourge that wisdom back to Hell,
> Which taught thee yet no better, that no pain

Can equal anger infinite provoked.
But wherefore thou alone? wherefore with thee
Came not all Hell broke loose? is pain to them
Less pain, less to be fled? or thou than they
Less hardy to endure? Courageous chief,
The first in flight from pain, hadst thou alleged
To thy deserted host this cause of flight,
Thou surely hadst not come sole fugitive."

To which the Fiend thus answered, frowning
stern:
"Not that I less endure, or shrink from pain,
Insulting Angel! well thou know'st I stood
They fiercest, when in battle to thy aid
The blasting vollied thunder made all speed,
And seconded thy else not dreaded spear.
But still thy words at random, as before,
Argue thy inexperience what behoves,
From hard assays and ill successes past,
A faithful leader; not to hazard all
Through ways of danger by himself untried.
I therefore, I alone, first undertook
To wing the desolate Abyss, and spy
This new-created World, whereof in Hell
Fame is not silent; here in hope to find
Better abode, and my afflicted powers
To settle here on Earth, or in mid air;
Though for possession put to try once more
What thou and thy gay legions dare against;
Whose easier business were to serve their Lord
High up in Heaven, with songs to hymn his throne,
And practised distances to cringe, not fight."

Satanic attack, particularly on monasteries and cathe-
drals, is much imagined, and Longfellow, in the prologue

234

to Part Two of *The Golden Legend*, dramatizes Lucifer in league with the Powers of the Air, making an assault on Strasbourg Cathedral. His objective is to tear the cross from the spire as well as hurl the bells to the ground, smash the casements and desecrate the dead.

[*Night and storm. Lucifer, with the Powers of the Air, trying to tear down the Cross.*]

LUCIFER

Hasten! Hasten!
O ye spirits!
From its station drag the ponderous
Cross of iron, that to mock us
Is uplifted high in air!

VOICES

Oh, we cannot!
For around it
All the Saints and Guardian Angels
Throng in legions to protect it;
They defeat us everywhere!

This assault on a consecrated building was very unique and showed a bravado (or desperation) that Lucifer had not been recorded as showing before. The voices of the Powers of the Air are more traditional in their acceptance of the impossible.

THE BELLS

Laudo Deum verum!
Plebem voco!
Congrego clerum!

Lucifer, however, was not abashed.

235

LUCIFER

Lower! lower!
Hover downward!
Seize the loud, vociferous bells, and
Clashing, clanging, to the pavement
Hurl them from their windy tower!

Neither, however, did the Powers of the Air lose their despondent note.

VOICES

All thy thunders
Here are harmless!
For these bells have been anointed,
And baptized with holy water!
They defy our utmost power.

THE BELLS

Defunctos ploro!
Pestem fugo!
Festa decoro!

Continuously, Lucifer exhorted his troops.

LUCIFER

Shake the casements!
Break the painted
Panes, that flame with gold and crimson;
Scatter them like leaves of Autumn,
Swept away before the blast!

But the Powers of the Air only replied that the principal Satanic adversary, the Archangel Michael, was now on the scene.

VOICES

O, we cannot!
The Archangel
Michael flames from every window,
With the sword of fire that drove us
Headlong, out of heaven, aghast!

THE BELLS

Funera Plango!
Fulgura frango!
Sabbata pango!

But in this poem, even St. Michael is not enough to quell
Lucifer's determination to destroy the cathedral.

LUCIFER

Aim your lightnings
At the oaken,
Massive, iron-studded portals!
Sack the house of God, and scatter
Wide the ashes of the dead!

And still the voices pleaded impotence:

VOICES

Oh, we cannot!
The Apostles
And the Martyrs, wrapped in mantles,
Stand as warders at the entrance,
Stand as sentinels o'erhead!

THE BELLS

Excito lentos!
Dissipo ventos!
Paco cruentos!

237

Finally, Lucifer, frustrated, howls his humiliation:

LUCIFER

Baffled! baffled!
Inefficient,
Craven spirits! leave this labor
Unto Time, the great Destroyer!
Come away, ere night is gone!

Suitably chastized, the Powers of the Air leave Strasbourg Cathedral, determined to persecute less formidable opponents.

VOICES

Onward! onward!
With the night-wind,
Over field and farm and forest,
Lonely homestead, darksome hamlet,
Blighting all we breathe upon!

A more earthbound version of the Devil appears in Dostoevski's *The Brothers Karamazov*. His character Ivan has a very strong sense of the earth's evil. Unable to bear the thought of being his father's murderer, he is overtaken by a bout of fever. In his delirium Ivan meets the Devil in person:

He was a gentleman, or rather a peculiarly Russian sort of gentleman, *qui frisait la cinquantaine*, going a little gray, with long thick hair and a pointed beard. He was wearing a brown jacket, well cut enough but already rather the worse for wear, at least three years old and thus completely out of fashion. His linen and his long cravat all spoke of the well-dressed man, but on closer inspection the linen revealed itself as of a dubious cleanliness, and the cravat as much soiled. His check trousers sat well on him, but they were too light and too close-fitting—the sort that nobody wears nowadays: his hat was a white felt one, quite out of keeping with the season. In short, a dandy fallen on bad times. He looked like one of those landed proprietors who flourished during the days of serfdom; he had lived in good society, but bit by bit, impoverished by his youthful dissipations and the recent abolition of serfdom, he had become a sort of high-class sponger, admitted into the society of his former acquaintances because of his pliable disposition, as a man one need not be ashamed to know, whom one can invite to meet anybody, only fairly far down the table. These hangers-s-on—compliant characters, good raconteurs, handy at the card table, unwilling social errand boys—are usually widowers or bachelors: Sometimes they have children, always brought up somewhere else, usually with some aunt or other whom the gentleman concerned never mentions in good company, as if the relationship embarrassed him. He ends up by losing contact with his children, who write to him from time to time (for his name day or Christmas) letters of congratulation which he sometimes answers and sometimes doesn't.

The expression of this unexpected guest was affable rather than friendly and obviously prepared for whatever politeness the situation might demand. He had no watch, but carried a tortoise-shell lorgnette on a black ribbon. A massive gold ring with a cheap opal adorned the middle finger of his right hand. Ivan Fyodorovich kept silent, determined that he for his part would not start the conversation. The visitor waited, like a poor relation who, arriving at teatime to provide company for the master of the house, finds him preoccupied with his thoughts and remains silent, ready nevertheless for polite conversation if his host initiates it.

A grim prophecy of hell on earth comes through the lips of Chigalev in *The Possessed*:

> Once the whole of humanity professes atheism—and I believe that this epoch will come in its turn, as inexorably as a geological period—then the old conception of the world will disappear of its own accord, without any cannibalism; and with it the old morality. Men will join together in drawing from life every possible enjoyment, but in this world alone. The human spirit will rise to a titanic pride, and this will be the deification of humanity. Triumphing ceaselessly and limitlessly over nature, by virtue of his knowledge and his power, man will experience thereby a joy so intense that it will replace for him the hope of heaven. Each will know that he is mortal, without hope of resurrection, and will resign himself to death with proud tranquillity, like a god. He will scorn in his pride to murmur at the shortness of life; he will love his brothers with an entirely disinterested love. Love itself will bring only passing joys, but the very knowledge of its transiency will deepen its intensity in proportion as it was once diluted by the hope of an eternal love beyond the tomb . . .

Byron talks of the Devil in *Manfred* and *Cain*, Baudelaire pleads with the Devil ("O Satan, take pity on my long wretchedness") and Victor Hugo provides Satan with redemption in his unfinished *La Fin de Satan*.

Shakespeare found the Devil to be a less fearful figure, and in *Twelfth Night* the Clown says to Malvolio, "Fie thou dishonest Satan! I call thee by the most modest terms: for I am one of those gentle ones that will use the devil himself with courtesy."

In *The Devil's Disciple*, George Bernard Shaw makes Satan a placating figure:

> You come to us from earth, full of the prejudices and terrors of that priest-ridden place. You have heard me ill spoken of; and yet, believe me, I have hosts of friends there.
>
> It is true—he continues—that the world cannot get on without me; but it never gives me credit for that: in its heart it mistrusts and hates me. Its sympathies are all with misery, with poverty, with starvation of the body and of the heart. I call on it to sympathize with joy, with love, with happiness, with beauty.

There are thousands of other references, of which these are a small selection. Robert Southey, in association with Coleridge, wrote this poem, entitled "The Devil's Walk":

> From his brimstone bed, at break of day
> A walking the Devil is gone,
> To look at his snug little farm of the world,
> And see how stock went on.
> How then was the Devil dressed?
> O, he was in his Sunday best;
> His coat was red, and his breeches were blue,
> And there was a hole where his tail came through.
> He passed a cottage with a double coach-house,
> A cottage of gentility!

241

And he owned with a grin
That his favourite sin
Is pride that apes humility.

Cynicism was Daniel Defoe's view:

> Wherever God erects a house of prayer,
> The Devil always builds a chapel there;
> And 'twill be found, upon examination,
> The latter has the largest congregation.

Belloc saw the Devil as all too vulnerable:

> The Devil, having nothing else to do,
> Went off to tempt my Lady Poltagrue.
> My Lady, tempted by a private whim,
> To his extreme annoyance, tempted him!

A more interior Devil was seen by John Davidson:

> I step into my heart and there I meet
> a god-almighty devil singing small,
> Who would like to shout and whistle in the street,
> And squelch the passers flat against the wall.

John Donne was more metaphysical:

> Go, and catch a falling star,
> Get with child a mandrake root,
> Tell me, where all past years are,
> Or who cleft the Devil's foot.

Christopher Marlowe took a universal view:

242

Unhappy spirits that fell with Lucifer,
Conspired against our God with Lucifer,
And are for ever damned with Lucifer

....

Hell hath no limits, nor is circumscribed
In one self place; for where we are is hell
And where hell is, must we ever be.

William Cowper saw the power of prayer as a deterrent
to Satan:

> Prayer makes the Christian's armour bright;
> And Satan trembles when he sees
> The weakest saint upon his knees.

Coleridge, however, saw demonism as sexually attractive and in "Kubla Khan" wrote:

> A savage place! As holy and enchanted
> As e'er beneath a waning moon was haunted
> By woman wailing for her demon lover.

In the "Ancient Mariner" he saw the Devil as man's
greatest foe:

> Like one, that on a lonesome road
> Doth walk in fear and dread,
> And having once turned round walks on,
> And turns no more his head;
> Because he knows, a frightful fiend
> Doth close behind him tread.

Elizabeth Barrett Browning saw Pan's demonic side as
highly destructive:

243

What was he doing, the great god Pan,
Down in the reeds by the river?
Spreading ruin, and scattering ban,
Splashing and paddling with hoofs of a goat,
And breaking the golden lilies afloat
With the dragon-fly on the river.

Again, hell could be created in the mind, as Milton pointed out in *Paradise Lost*:

The mind is its own place, and in itself
Can make a Heaven of Hell, a Hell of Heaven.

Kipling believed mankind has to tread a narrow path between hell—and hell:

A stone's throw on either hand
From that well-ordered road we tread,
And all the world is wild and strange:
Churel and ghoul and Djinn and sprite
Shall bear us company tonight,
For we have reached the Oldest Land
Wherein the Powers of Darkness range.

Personally, I think the most terrifyingly simplistic picture of hell emerges in an extract from Stella Gibbons' *Cold Comfort Farm*:

Ye know, doan't ye, what it feels like when ye burn your hand in takin' a cake out of the oven or wi' a match when ye're lightin' one of they godless cigarettes? Aye, it stings wi' a fearful pain, doan't it? And ye run away to clap a bit o' butter on it to take the pain away. Ah but (an impressive pause) *there'll be no butter in hell!*

Much of demonic art has been highly detailed and some of it is illustrated in this book. Nothing underlines this preoccupation with demonic minutiae than the following extract from the Lalita Vistara, which describes the attack of Mara, the Devil of tantric Buddhism on the redeemer Bodhisattva:

> The devil Papiyan [Mara] . . . prepared his mighty army, four legion strong and valiant in combat, a fearful army that struck terror into the hearts of all who beheld it, an army such as had never been seen or heard of before, by men or gods. This army had the power to take on all manner of different appearances, transforming itself endlessly in a hundred million ways.

The description of this grotesque host is very similar to the medieval style of satanic painting. For instance, the body of the formidable army was wrapped in the coils of a hundred thousand serpents, and in its hands were swords, bows, arrows, pikes, axes, mallets, rockets, pestles, sticks, chains, clubs, discuses and numerous other instruments of war. The hands and feet of this extraordinary army turned in all directions while its body was protected with breastplates. The troops' eyes and faces were flaming and each soldier had enormous dog's teeth. Some spat the venom of snakes and some ate it. Others ate human flesh, blood, feet, hands, heads, livers, entrails and bones. Some had bodies of black, bluish, red and yellow flame, while others had hollow, inflamed, gouged or squinting eyes.

245

One battalion carried burning mountains, another (more modestly) torn-up tree roots. One group had the ears of pigs, elephants or boars, while another had no ears at all. Another group had stomachs like mountains, some had stomachs like rounded jars, feet like the feet of cranes, skin and flesh and blood dried up and their ears, noses, hands, feet, eyes and heads all lopped off. Other troops were equally colorful.

> Some with the skin of oxen, asses, boars, ichneumons, stags, rams, beetles, cats, apes, wolves, and jackals, were spitting snake venom, and—swallowing balls of fire, breathing flame, sending down a rain of brass and molten iron, calling up black clouds, bringing black night, and making a great noise— were running toward the Bodhisattva. . . .

This kind of demonic style is well epitomized by Hieronymus Bosch, who is typical of the problems of unrealism that dogged the fifteenth century, caught as it was between the faith of medieval times and the beginnings of modern rationalism. In the "Temptation of St. Anthony" the invasion of the fortress where St. Anthony sought solitude is depicted. The witches' sabbat, the lakeside satanist meeting, the Devil's pact, the black mass—all are there. In his painting "The Last Judgment," a triptych in the Vienna Academy of Fine Arts, the drama is heightened. Infernal monsters roam the earth, a sky of horror lights a background of burning buildings, and the elements of hell are ready to seize their prey. Within the complexity of the painting, men are being burned alive, hung, throttled and quartered. Tortures include the wheel, the water torture and the millstone. Lemurs leap from the depths, a devil flies on the back of a witch and satanic creatures proliferate.

Very much in the same style as Bosch is Breughel the Elder. "The Fall of the Rebel Angels" represents the hurling of the damned from the heavenly heights to the burning floor of hell. In "Dulle Griet," in the Musée Mayer van den Bergh in Antwerp, the damnation of mankind is seen in a broader concept. A shipwreck is on the horizon, plague-stricken groups are locked in battle, and the details include the pitiless mower, gibbets and assassins.

In Christian art the Devil appears in many forms. He is carved on choir benches, entwined on columns, and stares from bas-reliefs. In the medieval churches he is usually seen as a serpent with a human face. In Europe he is also seen as a bull, or a bear, or a leopard, although he is also represented in human form.

Here are a selection of the most dramatic artistic sightings:

1. *Byzantine monasteries around Mount Athos in Greece*: Satan is painted with an enormous mouth and huge teeth. He is seen eating sinners, standing in a pool of fire, while his sinful fodder lies in the bloodied depths of the pool.

2. *Walls of Camposanto in Italy*: There are many fiendish shapes painted on these walls, including Satan sitting in hell with three mouths. In his claws he grasps sinners, while the mouths devour them.

3. *Tower of Notre Dame in Paris:* Here the Devil is seen winged, with lolling tongue, horns and a particularly malevolent expression.

4. *Bodleian Library in Oxford:* On stained glass Satan is seen as a beautiful woman tempting St. Dunstan.

5. *Bourges Cathedral in France:* Both hell and the last judgment are sculptured here, populated by a profusion of diabolical figures.

Among illustrated manuscripts or books there are thousands of satanic images. But perhaps the two most outstanding are the twelfth-century *Hortus Deliciarum* and some of the illustrations to Dante's *Inferno*. The *Hortus Deliciarum* was written for the edification of monks, and the devilish temptations illustrated in it include city life, lavish dress, laziness, money and worldly goods. The Devil is seen as a dragon or griffin, with lolling tongue, prehensile claws and enormous sable wings. He is accompanied by demonic cats and bestiary, while skulls and the artifacts of the charnel house surround him.

In the illustrations to Dante's *Inferno*, Satan is again seen to be triple-headed, cannibalistic and voraciously eating Cassius, Brutus (Caesar's assassins) and Judas Iscariot. He is also seen as a winged satyr with a magic horn, a half-human figure with the tusks of a swine guarding a treasure hoard, and as a bound prisoner, writhing amid dwarflike satellites. One particularly dramatic illustration shows him enthroned in gloom, surrounded by shrieking hags and glamorous initiates. The setting is a sinister forest grove and littered around it are the skulls and the gangrenous, half-masticated limbs of sacrificial infants.

Albrecht Dürer produced a number of satanic paintings, including "Knight, Death and the Devil," "The Four Witches," "Key of the Bottomless Pit" and the engraving "Death and the Devil." Another version of the Temptation of St. Anthony was painted by Stefano al Giovanni Sassetta and called "St. Anthony Tormented by Demons." It shows the saint lying helplessly on the ground, while he is lashed by strange birdlike tormentors. He is surrounded by funereal trees and is being approached by dark, shaggy creatures holding writhing snakes in their hands.

Finally, another demonically impressive painter is Goya. His themes included fiends, warlocks, ghouls, witches, necromancers and demonry. He created his own, very individual occult world peopled by its own, horrific creatures. Corpses rise from graves, goat-shaped demons gambol in baleful darkness, sexual witches fly through the darkness, and the rites of the Sabbat are celebrated with spectral glee. "The Gathering of the Sorcerers" is typical of his work. A goatlike Satan sits enthroned, surrounded by witches, against the background of dark clouds and a crescent moon. An emaciated child is sprawled on the ground while a witch is presenting another child to the Devil as a sacrifice.

William Blake shows the conflict between Good and Evil but in a much more poetic and less demonic light. The same applies to the nineteenth-century painter Gustav Doré, who depicts Satan winged and with hands outstretched, sitting in an ebony-pillared chamber. He is addressing his hordes of demons and, equipped with Stygian wings, they stand in martial formation. In another Doré painting, "Sovereign of the Infernal Hosts," Satan is shown among his legions. Doré sees him here as a dominating winged creature, flying over a whirling universe.

Bosch, Breughel the Elder and Goya are probably the most demonic of Satan's illustrators and they certainly show the greatest and the darkest imagination. With the coming of the nineteenth century, the medieval style in all its black majesty and grotesque form disappeared. The shadowy hosts, contorted fiends and sexual horror were gone and a more philosophical mood emerged. But more profound as this was, the real satanic masterpieces belong to a much earlier age.

PART NINE

The Devil's Advocates

Christian, dost thou see them
On the holy ground,
How the troops of Midian
Prowl and prowl around?

Hymns Ancient and Modern

Satan possesses great courage, incredible cunning, superhuman wisdom, the most acute penetration, consummate prudence, an incomparable skill in veiling the most pernicious artifices under a specious disguise, and a malicious and infinite hatred towards the human race, implacable and incurable.

Johann Weyer, *De Praestigiis Daemorium*

It has emerged clearly from this book that the old biblical and medieval concept of hell as being a bottomless pit somewhere below us is quite wrong. Hell is here on earth and is with us all the time in a dualistic way with God. Freud said:

> God is a father-substitute, or, more correctly, an exalted father, or yet again, a reproduction of the father as seen and met with in childhood. . . . It requires no great analytic insight to divine that God and the Devil were originally one and the same, a single figure which was later split into two bearing opposed characteristics. . . . The father is thus the individual prototype of both God and the Devil.

The main reason why there has been such a growth of interest and involvement in the occult and in the satanic throughout the 1960s and so far into the 1970s has been the spiritual sterility of the established Church. Because of this, thousands, needing spirituality, needing an object of faith, have turned to Zen, Hare Krishna, Yoga, drugs and satanism. The most regular accusation against the clergy is that they do not talk enough about God, that they enshroud the Christian message with simplistic homily or ludicrous, intelligence-insulting comparisons, or they inadequately modernize ritual so that all spiritualism is discharged. In this context, therefore, the true but unwitting group of Devil's advocates are the clergy of the established Churches themselves. Father Kenneth Leech in *The Real Jesus Revolution* makes the significant comment that: ". . . religion is on the increase everywhere, perhaps, except *inside* the Church."

John Kerr wrote in *The Mystery and Magic of the Occult:*

> The Church is becoming profoundly unspiritual, even a little ashamed of religion as such. The occult

craze ought to tell the ecclesiastical powers that even though their institutions are in trouble, religion as such is once again in the mainstream.

A major satanist such as Crowley was obviously looking for his own form of spirituality as were his followers. Crowley created a black fantasy-world for them, eventually emerging himself as faithless as when he created his own religion. Manson was also looking for a form of spirituality—as were *his* followers. Manson's creation had infinitely darker and more savage results than Crowley's. Equally all the other satanists, the witches and those who feared or created them and many of those who were possessed were all looking for a faith that the church, involved in its own politics or misguided campaigns, was clearly unable to give them.

In many ways, the Church has been complacent about the synthetic black and white rulings concerning the wonder and tranquillity of heaven—as opposed to the fire and brimstone of hell, or the just, loving, but vengeance-seeking God—as opposed to the devious, soul-snaring and sadistic Devil. Hell has always been sharply defined by the Church but heaven rarely detailed. Little indication of forgiveness for Satan as a Fallen Angel appears in the Bible. Isaiah, in Chapter 14, Verses 12–15, predicting the downfall of the King of Babylon, says:

How are thou fallen from heaven, O Lucifer, son of the morning! How art thou cut down to the ground, which didst weaken the nations! For thou hast said in thine heart, I will ascend unto heaven, I will exalt my throne above the Stars of God: I will sit also upon the mount of the congregation, in the sides of the north: I will ascend above the heights of the clouds; I will be like the most High. Yet thou shalt be brought down to hell, to the sides of the pit.

The established Church has leaned heavily on both the Old and New Testament warnings against occult practice in general. The Old Testament condemnation is contained in Deuteronomy, Chapter 18, Verses 9–14:

When you come into the land which the Lord your God is giving you, do not learn to imitate the abominable customs of those other nations. Let no one be found among you who makes his son or daughter pass through fire, no augur or soothsayer or diviner or sorcerer, no one who casts spells or traffics with ghosts or spirits, and no necromancer. Those who do these things are abominable to the Lord your God, and it is because of these abominable practises that the Lord your God is driving them out before you. You shall be wholehearted in your service of the Lord your God. These nations whose place you are taking listen to soothsayers and augurs, but the Lord your God does not permit you to do this.

The New Testament takes an equally firm stand against occult practice, and Chapter 19, Verses 18–20, in the Acts of the Apostles reads:

Some believers, too, came forward to admit in detail how they had used spells and a number of them who had practised magic collected their books and made a bonfire of them in public. The value of these was calculated to be fifty thousand silver pieces. In this impressive way the world of the Lord spread more and more widely and successfully.

In his report on exorcism, the Bishop of Exeter stated that:

> In western countries today, the widespread apostasy from the Christian faith, accompanied by an increasing recourse to black magic and occult practises, is revealing the presence and the power of evil forces.

The mind can create what is understood by Satan and his forces quite easily from dabbling with the occult although like any other ancient science, the occult is yielding up its secrets and making a genuine contribution to research. This is particularly true in the cases of ESP and telekinisis and has been true in the past in the cases of astrology and palmistry. Psychic phenomena in general have often been dismissed by the Church, mainly because the clergy are only interested in eternal life. It is only the appearance of priests like Martin Israel who shed a ray of hope and light over the Churches' association with the psychical. The occultist will need to manipulate the future, and this can be done by divination from a large number of preachers. Christian teaching insists that faith will determine the future, and Chapter 6, Verses 31–34, of Matthew categorically state:

> So do not worry; do not say "What are we to eat? What are we to drink? How are we to be clothed?" It is the pagans who set their hearts on all these things. Your heavenly Father knows you need them all. Set your hearts on his kingdom first, and on his righteousness, and all these other things will be given you as well. So do not worry about tomorrow.

The satanist likes to be master of his own destiny, although this has more or less always ended in a far greater misery and disaster than anyone involved in practicing Christianity. Another significant and rather forbidding fact is that intense interest in the occult has often preceded catastrophe not just involving personal disaster but national. Satanism and occultism was practiced in Berlin and Munich between the two World Wars. Sensuality, drug-taking, sexual exploitation of every kind was the order of the day, while hypnotists, mediums, fortune-tellers and astrologers abounded in person as well as in print.

John Richards in his book *But Deliver Us From Evil* agrees that occultism is a demonic omen and writes:

Nazism serves as a recent and vivid reminder that the occult-ridden society is no new thing, and that such a society, far from being powerful, becomes increasingly vulnerable to the destructive powers among those it hopes to manipulate. The main reason for drawing attention to the occult and demonic in the past is to enable us to see the true nature of the present.

The satanic components and more contemporary practice assembled in this book are certainly designed not only to illustrate the true nature of present interest in the Devil but also to show how strong demonic faith has been and continues to be. The Devil's dominion is very wide and gains strength from the spiritual weakness of the Church. It is important to remember that the Witchcraft Act of 1737 was not repealed until 1951 and that in many parts of the world, worship of the Devil, in various forms, is still very much in evidence.

> My sweet Lord, I really want to feel you
> I really want to be with you

sang George Harrison. These two lines exactly sum up current feeling. The need for faith is desperate and the Church, despite numerous efforts, cannot provide centralization of belief. A visit to the majority of Church services will confirm that. Evangelists claim they experience a turning point—a revelation of God—and they are anxious to go out into the world and save souls. But more often than not they turn would-be seekers of faith away from God by their bland complacency, narrow views and oversimplifications.

The greatest tragedy is the sheer unexploitation of the Church's spiritual potential. This potential is the greatest weapon against the demonaics of the mind. The only way it can be realized is to return to the great mysticism of God and the miracle of creation. Once this factor is intelligently and perceptively preached, then the world's spiritual needs can be resolved—and the Devil's dominion will no longer hold sway.

SELECTIVE BIBLIOGRAPHY

Unless otherwise noted, place of publication is London.

Baker, Roger. *Binding the Devil.* Sheldon Press, 1974.

Baskin, Wade. *Dictionary of Satanism.* New York: Citadel Press, 1972.

Boon, Martin (Editor). *Exorcism: Fact Not Fiction.* New York: New American Library, 1974.

Branston, Brian. *Beyond Belief.* Weidenfeld & Nicolson, 1973.

Bugliosi, Vincent with Gentry, Curt. *Helter Skelter.* The Bodley Head, 1975.

Cavendish, Richard. *The Black Arts.* Routledge & Kegan Paul, 1967.

———. *The Powers of Evil in Western Religion, Magic and Folk Belief.* Routledge & Kegan Paul, 1975.

Chaundler, Christine. *Every Man's Book of Superstitions.* Mowbray, 1932.

Chesney, Kellow. *The Victorian Underworld.* Temple Smith, 1975.

Cohn, Norman. *Europe's Inner Demons.* Paladin, 1975.

Defoe, Daniel. *The History of the Devil.* E. P. Publishing, 1892.

Deutch, Richard. *Exorcism, Possession or Obsession?* Bachman and Turner, 1975.

Duffy, Maureen. *The Erotic World of Faery.* Hodder & Stoughton, 1975.

Ebon, Martin. *Exorcism Past and Present.* Cassell, 1974.

Encyclopedia of Witchcraft and Demonology. Octopus, 1974.

Fort, Charles. *The Book of the Damned.* New York: Abacus, 1941.

Greaves, Helen. *The Wheel of Eternity.* Neville Spearman, 1969.

Haining, Peter. *The Necromancers.* Hodder & Stoughton, 1972.

———. *Ghosts: The Illustrated History.* Sidgwick & Jackson, 1974.

———. *Witchcraft and Black Magic.* Hamlyn, 1974.

Haining, Peter (Editor). *The Black Magic Omnibus Vol. 1.* Robson, 1976.

———. *The Black Magic Omnibus Vol. 2.* Robson, 1976.

Hartley, Christine. *The Western Mystery Tradition.* The Aquarian Press, 1968.

Hontheim, Father Joseph. *The Catholic Encyclopedia.* 1903.

Huxley, Julian. *The Devils of Loudun.* Chatto and Windus, 1932.

Israel, Martin. *Precarious Living.* Hodder & Stoughton, 1976.

Johnson, Paul. *A History of Christianity.* Weidenfeld & Nicolson, 1977.

Kerr, John. *The Mystery & Magic of the Occult.* 1953.

Landsbury, Alan. *In Search of Magic and Witchcraft.* Corgi, 1977.

Leech, Father Kenneth. *The Real Jesus.* [?], 1973.

Lévi, Eliphas, translated by Crowley, Aleister. *The Key of the Mysteries.* Rider, 1947.

Lindsey, Hal, with Carlson, C. C. *Satan Is Alive and Well on Planet Earth.* New York: Zondervan, 1972.

Maple, Eric. *The Dark World of Witches.* Pan, 1968.

Milton, John. *Paradise Lost.* Cambridge, 1894.

Morley, John. *Death, Heaven and the Victorians.* Studio Vista, 1963.

Murray, Margaret Alice. *God of the Witches.* Sampson Low, 1932.

Neil-Smith, Christopher. *The Exorcist and the Possessed.* James Pike, 1974.

Paine, Lauran. *The Hierarchy of Hell.* Hale, 1972.

Parker, Derek and Julia. *The Immortals.* Barrie and Jenkins, 1976.

Pearce-Higgins, Canon J. D. and Whitby, Rev. G. Stanley. *Life, Death and Psychical Research.* Rider, 1973.

Petitpierre, Dom Robert O.S.B. *Exorcising Devils.* Robert Hale, 1972.

Richards, John. *But Deliver Us From Evil. An introduction to the demonic dimension in pastoral care.* Darton, Longman & Todd, 1974.

259

Rowell, Geoffrey. *Hell and the Victorians.* Oxford, 1975.

Sargant, William. *The Mind Possessed.* Heinemann, 1973.

———. *Battle for the Mind.* Heinemann, 1957.

———. *The Unquiet Mind.* Heinemann, 1967.

Seligman, Kurt. *Magic, Supernaturalism and Religion.* Paladin, 1969.

Shah, Idries. *The Secret Lore of Magic.* Muller, 1937.

Sheed, F. J. (Editor). *Soundings in Satanism.* New York: Mowbrays, 1972.

Singer, Kurt (Editor). *They Are Possessed.* W. H. Allen, 1970.

Symonds, John. *The Great Beast. The Life and Magick of Aleister Crowley.* Macdonald, 1973.

Wedeck, Harry E. *The Triumph of Satan.* New York: Citadel Press, 1970.

Wilson, Colin. *The Occult.* Hodder and Stoughton, 1974.

Wilson, Colin (Editor). *Men of Mystery.* Star, 1977.

Woods, William. *A History of the Devil.* W. H. Allen, 1973.

INDEX

263